Start Your Own Business!

For over twenty-five hundred years, *The Art of War* has helped its readers find **competitive advantage** using the secrets of Sun Tzu. In this adaptation, we apply these ancient secrets to starting a business. *The Art of Starting a Business* covers the complete strategy you need to create a successful new enterprise.

- Business planning
- Making a profit
- Marketing
- Making sales
- Customer relationships
- Business stages

This volume contains **two books.** It contains **the complete text** of Sun Tzu's *The Art of War.* It also contains a detailed, line-by-line adaptation called *The Art of Starting a Business.* This adaptation applies Sun Tzu's immortal advice specifically to starting a business.

This book is only the beginning

This book also contains **the secret password keys** that allow you to access *The Warrior Class*, the world's largest site for on-line training in Sun Tzu's methods (see **www.clearbridge.com** for information). This site contains hundred of pages of training material to help you master Sun Tzu's techniques. This material is **FREE** to the owners of this book.

Buy this book today and study its ideas forever!

Other *Art of War* Works from Clearbridge Publishing

The Art of War *Plus* Sun Tzu's Own Words
(ISBN 1929194005)
The Art of War *Plus* The Art of Sales
(ISBN 1929194013)
The Art of War *Plus* The Art of Management
(ISBN 1929194056)
The Art of War *Plus* The Art of Marketing
(ISBN 1929194021)
The Art of War *Plus*
The Amazing Secrets of Sun Tzu
(ISBN 1929194072)
The Art of War *Plus* The Warrior Class
(ISBN 1929194099)
The Art of War *Plus* The Art of Career Building
(ISBN 1929194137)
The Amazing Secrets of Sun Tzu THE VIDEO SEMINAR
(ISBN 1929194110)
The Amazing Secrets of Sun Tzu THE AUDIO SEMINAR
(ISBN 1929194129)

Sun Tzu's
The Art of War
Plus
The Art of
Starting a Business

孫
子
兵
法

To my business partner and wife, Rebecca

Sun Tzu's
The Art of War
Plus
The Art of
Starting a Business

By
Gary Gagliardi

Clearbridge Publishing

Published by
Clearbridge Publishing

FIRST EDITION
Copyright 1999, 2002 © Gary Gagliardi

Manufactured in the United States of America
Front Cover Art by Gary Gagliardi
Back Cover photograph by Rebecca Gagliardi

Library of Congress Control Number: 2002090340
ISBN 1-929194-15-3
Clearbridge Publishing's books may be purchased for business, for any promotional use, or for special sales. Please contact:

Clearbridge PUBLISHING
P.O. Box 33772, Shoreline, WA 98133
Phone: (206)-533-9357 Fax: (206)546-9756
www.clearbridge.com
info@clearbridge.com

CONTENTS

How to Use This Book

This is a different type of book on starting a business. It won't tell you how to write a business plan or rent an office. It doesn't deal with incorporation or filing taxes. There are plenty of other books about those topics.

This book instead addresses the strategic philosophy of creating a new business. It is about picking the right customers, the importance of making a profit, and how to make your business more competitive. More importantly, as a guide to starting a business, it directly adapts the world's best book on strategy, Sun Tzu's _The Art of War_ to the problems of a new business.

For over two thousand years, people have treasured Sun Tzu's famous treatise on war for one reason: its competitive methods work extremely well. As the first of the military classics, _The Art of War_ offers a distinct, non-intuitive philosophy on how to discover the path to success. This philosophy works in any dynamic environment where people find themselves contesting with one another for a specific goal.

This book on using Sun Tzu's methods for starting a business grew directly out of our other business books based on _The Art of War_. We had already published books adapting Sun Tzu's techniques to sales, marketing, and management, but people starting a new business must master all of these specific skills and more. For them, we developed this special version that wraps all of these skills together and adds everything else I wish I had known when I started my first business.

In addressing the question about whether or not Sun Tzu's methods work in building a business, I can only depend on my own experience. Before I discovered _The Art of War_, I tried starting two businesses. The first consumed money for almost two years before we closed it down. The second fell apart and was sold within a year. After I started studying and using Sun Tzu's methods, the next business that I started went on to become one of the Inc. 500 fastest growing privately owned businesses in America.

This book offers the complete text of *The Art of War* plus a line-by line adaptation applying Sun Tzu's lessons to the challenges of starting a business. In reading *The Art of War* and *The Art of Starting a Business* side-by-side, I encourage you to think about your own problems in creating a new business and *make notes* about how to apply Sun Tzu's suggestions to your own situation.

Even in applying *The Art of War* specifically to starting a business, you will draw different lessons from the text depending on your situation when you read it. For this reason, we recommend that when starting a business, you reread this book every six months or so to keep your strategy on track.

Why should Sun Tzu's philosophy of warfare apply so well to the problems of starting a business? It works because all competition, including the competition for customers, arises from the same factors. Sun Tzu wrote about human nature, the issues of choice, and what matters in winning against the competition. The nature of competition hasn't changed in the last two thousand years and it won't over the next two thousand. The only differences between business competition and warfare are the types of tools we use and the nature of the battleground.

Sun Tzu realized that competition is, by nature, a chaotic system. He used the term "chaos" in a surprisingly modern, scientific sense. He did not mean that competitive systems don't have structure. He meant that they are complex, self-organizing systems from which patterns naturally emerge but in which it is very difficult to predict or control specific events. Those who wish to understand the true nature of competition are well served studying modern chaos theory. If you do, you will discover that many of its principles were uncovered by Sun Tzu twenty-five hundred years ago.

People mistakenly see war and, more generally, competition as an adversarial, destructive process, but Sun Tzu saw competition as a necessary component of a productive world. He saw competition as costly but not necessarily destructive. He was familiar with the potentially destructive nature of war, but he teaches us how to minimize the costs of competition through logic and persuasion. He taught methods that avoid the most costly forms of conflict and yet allow us to win new positions and territory.

This approach works equally well in winning customers and making a profit. From Sun Tzu, we learn how to discover new market positions, how to work with and sell to customers, and how to be successful at minimal risk. We learn how to continually improve processes and increase productivity.

As you read this book, notice how closely *The Art of Starting a Business* follows Sun Tzu's original ideas in *The Art of War*. While *The Art of Starting a Business* applies Sun Tzu's ideas in ways that he would never have foreseen, it does so respecting the integrity of his thinking. I truly don't think of these career advancement ideas as my own, but as interpretations of Sun Tzu's approach to successful competition. I follow his advice and admonitions as closely as possible, line-by-line.

When we adapt Sun Tzu's methods from warfare to business, the lessons that emerge from Sun Tzu are intriguing. Sun Tzu teaches first that generating business is not enough. The goal is to win business easily, at a profit, with minimal risk. The first step in planning a business is understanding our strengths and weaknesses versus those of the competition. We want to fight for a business only in situations where we are certain to win. We also want to be certain that winning is well worth the cost.

Next, Sun Tzu's lessons are extremely specific about what to do in certain situations. He wants us to pay close attention to the details of our business situation. He enumerates different business stages, different types of opponents, different decision-making mistakes, different competitive signals, and so on. Although Sun Tzu wrote twenty-five hundred years ago about warfare, when adapted to starting a business, these detailed lists are still surprisingly complete. Their advice is useful to anyone planning their career.

Next, Sun Tzu offers his "cooperative" view of competition. In his system, we cannot win through our own actions. We don't create business opportunities. We can only discover new opportunities when needs in the marketplace create them. The secret is recognizing a good opportunity when it presents itself. The knowledge of how to run a certain type of business is not enough. We must always look for customer needs that others are not addressing in the marketplace. We must let the needs of customers shape our business if we want to make a success of it.

Finally, Sun Tzu's view of competition is knowledge-intensive. He sees victory going to the person who is the most knowledgeable. He even recognizes creativity as a special and important type of knowledge. Business innovation and continual improvement flow naturally from his philosophy. In Sun Tzu, there is no substitute for good information. We are beginning to realize that people in the economy are paid for their knowledge, but knowledge in Sun Tzu's system is more than a higher degree of skill. Knowledge means having better information than anyone else, ideally, knowing more about our area of business than any of our competitors know.

This version of *The Art of War* is just one of many versions and adaptations offered by Clearbridge Publishing. We have or will develop versions for every common form of competition in modern life. We suggest you visit **www.clearbridge.com** for a complete list of our current titles.

For further in-depth study of Sun Tzu's methods, we have created *The Warrior Class*, our on-line training center, which contains hundred of slides, text lessons, and tests to help people master Sun Tzu. Access to the on-line site is FREE to anyone buying our books. See **www.clearbridge.com** for more information on accessing *The Warrior Class*.

Gary Gagliardi, 2002

PLANNING

This is war.
It is the most important skill in the nation.
It is the basis of life and death.
It is the philosophy of survival or destruction.
You must know it well.

Your skill comes from five factors.
Study these factors when you plan war.
You must insist on knowing the nature of:
1. military philosophy,
2. the weather,
3. the ground,
4. the commander,
5. and military methods.

It starts with your military philosophy.
Command your people in a way that gives them a higher
shared purpose.
You can lead them to death.
You can lead them to life.
They must never fear danger or dishonesty.

PLANNING A BUSINESS

Starting a business is a challenge.
It is requires every skill that you have.
You determine whether or not the new business survives.
The business determines your success or failure.
You must understand exactly what you are doing.

Five factors decide your business's initial success.
Evaluate these factors when planning your business.
You must know:
1. your business purpose,
2. the economic trends,
3. your target market,
4. your skills,
5. and your business operating procedures.

Your business begins with your purpose.
Organize your business so that it satisfies a well-defined need.
Your business can hurt people.
Your business can give them a better life.
Your people must never fear danger or dishonesty.

Next, you have the weather.
It can be sunny or overcast.
It can be hot or cold.
It includes the timing of the seasons.

Next is the terrain.
It can be distant or near.
It can be difficult or easy.
It can be open or narrow.
It also determines your life or death.

Next is the commander.
He must be smart,
trustworthy,
caring,
brave,
and strict.

Finally, you have your military methods.
They include the shape of your organization.
This comes from your management philosophy.
You must master their use.

All five of these factors are critical.
As a commander, you must pay attention to them.
Understanding them brings victory.
Ignoring them means defeat.

Next are the economic trends.
The business climate can change from good to bad.
Your business can go from hot to cold.
The economic trends will change with time.

Next is your target market.
It can be distant or near.
It can be difficult or easy to contact.
It can be large or small.
Your target market determines your success or failure.

Next are your skills.
You must be a visionary,
an accountant,
an enthusiast,
a sales person,
and a manager.

Finally, you need defined business operating procedures.
You must organize the work so that it creates value.
Your procedures depend upon your philosophy.
You must master effectiveness and efficiency.

All five factors are important.
You must pay attention to them all.
Your choices here determine your success.
You will fail if you take any of them for granted.

You must learn through planning.
You must question the situation.

You must ask:
Which government has the right philosophy?
Which commander has the skill?
Which season and place have the advantage?
Which method of command works?
Which group of forces has the strength?
Which officers and men have the training?
Which rewards and punishments make sense?
This tells when you will win and when you will lose.
Some commanders perform this analysis.
If you use these commanders, you will win.
Keep them.
Some commanders ignore this analysis.
If you use these commanders, you will lose.
Get rid of them.

Plan an advantage by listening.
This makes you powerful.
Get assistance from the outside.
Know the situation.
Then planning can creates advantages and controls power.

You need to learn and analyze each business factor.
You must constantly question your assumptions.

You must ask:
What is the real purpose for my business?
Do I have the needed skills?
When and where can I create additional value?
How should my business be organized?
How is my business going to beat the competition?
Why does my business do the work more effectively?
Do my pricing and products make sense?
This analysis tells whether or not a business can succeed.
You must ask these question over and over again.
If you strengthen your plan, you will be successful.
Keep at it.
Most people don't perform this careful analysis.
They think they will succeed just by working hard.
This is why 80% of new businesses fail.

Planning forces you to listen to other people.
The more you know, the stronger your business will be.
Get help from those who know your industry.
Know the reality of the situation.
Planning uncovers opportunities and focuses your energies.

Warfare is one thing.
It is a philosophy of deception.

When you are ready, you try to appear incapacitated.
When active, you pretend inactivity.
When you are close to the enemy, you appear distant.
When far away, pretend you are near.

If the enemy has strong position, entice him away from it.
If the enemy is confused, be decisive.
If the enemy is solid, prepare against him.
If the enemy is strong, avoid him.
If the enemy is angry, frustrate him.
If the enemy is weak, make him arrogant.
If the enemy is relaxed, make him work.
If the enemy is united, break him apart.
Attack him when he is unprepared.
Leave when he least expects it.

You will find a place where you can win.
Don't pass it by.

Success in business requires one thing.
You must control people's perceptions.

If you are new, you must appear experienced.
If business is slow, you must appear busy.
If you are anxious, you must appear calm.
If you are worried, you must appear enthusiastic.

If competitors have a good idea, take it as your own.
When customers are uncertain, help them decide.
When competitors are good, you must be better.
When competitors are strong, find a different business.
If customer decisions are emotional, play to emotion.
If competitors are weak, make them overconfident.
If competitors win easy sales, make them work for them.
If competitors have partners, steal the partners away.
Go after competitors who don't expect competition.
Avoid competing in ways that competitors expect.

You will find an opportunity that assures profit.
Never pass it by.

Before you go to war, you must believe that you can count
on victory.

You must calculate many advantages.

Before you go to battle, you may believe that you can foresee
defeat.

You can count few advantages.

Many advantages add up to victory.

Few advantages add up to defeat.

How can you know your advantages without analyzing them?

We can see where we are by means of our observations.

We can foresee our victory or defeat by planning.

Before starting a business, you must know that you can make a profit.

Profit measures the unique value you add to a product.

Before wasting your efforts, you must avoid doing business that isn't profitable.

Your work can add too little value to your product.

Many sources of profit add up to success.

Few sources of profit add up to failure.

How can you know what is profitable without analysis?

You must know the value you add by measuring profits.

You can foresee success or failure by planning.

GOING TO WAR

Everything depends on your use of military philosophy.
Moving the army requires thousands of vehicles.
These vehicles must be loaded thousands of times.
The army must carry a huge supply of arms.
You need ten thousand acres of grain.
This results in internal and external shortages.
Any army consumes resources like an invader.
It uses up glue and paint for wood.
It requires armor for its vehicles.
People complain about the waste of a vast amount of metal.
It will set you back when you raise tens of thousands of
troops.

Using a large army makes war very expensive to win.
Long delays create a dull army and sharp defeats.
Attacking enemy cities drains your forces.
Long campaigns that exhaust the nation's resources are
wrong.

Making a Profit

Everything depends on your business's purpose.
Creating a business requires thousands of ideas.
These ideas must be tested over and over.
The business requires a good supply of products.
You need thousands of dollars in capital.
Your family and your business will be short of money.
A new business consumes resources like a thief.
It consumes your time and energy.
You must defend your decisions.
People will complain about the money you've spent.
It costs too much if you try to hire lots of people to start your business.

Employees make it difficult to make a profit.
A slow start creates a dull business that isn't profitable.
Competing against an entrenched competitor is expensive.
Taking a long time to make a profit drains your resources and is wrong.

Manage a dull army.
You will suffer sharp defeats.
Drain your forces.
Your money will be used up.
Your rivals multiply as your army collapses and they will begin
against you.
It doesn't matter how smart you are.
You cannot get ahead by taking losses!

You hear of people going to war too quickly.
Still, you won't see a skilled war that lasts a long time.

You can fight a war for a long time or you can make your
nation strong.
You can't do both.

You can never totally understand all the dangers in using
arms.
Therefore, you can never totally understand the advantages in
using arms either.

You want to make good use of war.
Do not raise troops repeatedly.
Do not carry too many supplies.
Choose to be useful to your nation.
Feed off the enemy.
Make your army carry only the provisions it needs.

Build a sluggish business.
You will lose money consistently.
It drains your energy.
Your capital will be used up.
Your business will collapse and competitors will start up against you.
It doesn't matter how smart you think you are.
You can't get ahead by losing money.

You can sometimes make a profit too quickly.
However, no good business loses money for a long time.

You can support a losing business for a long time or make your family happy.
You can't do both at once.

8—

You can never completely insure against failure when you start a business.
It follows that you can never know all the opportunities in a business either.

You must make good use of your business investment.
Do not raise money repeatedly.
Do not stock too much inventory.
Choose to be valuable to your family.
Sell your products.
Invest only in the items you absolutely need.

8—

The nation impoverishes itself shipping to troops that are far
away.
Distant transportation is costly for hundreds of families.
Buying goods with the army nearby is also expensive.
These high prices also impoverish hundreds of families.
People quickly exhaust their resources supporting a military
force.
Military forces consume a nation's wealth entirely.
War leaves households in the former heart of the nation with
nothing.

War destroys hundreds of families.
Out of every ten families, war leaves only seven.
War empties the government's storehouses.
Broken armies will get rid of their horses.
They will throw down their armor, helmets, and arrows.
They will lose their swords and shields.
They will leave their wagons without oxen.
War will consume sixty percent of everything you have.

Because of this, the commander's duty is to feed off the
enemy.

Use a cup of the enemy's food.
It is worth twenty of your own.
Win a bushel of the enemy's feed.
It is worth twenty of your own.

You can kill the enemy and frustrate him as well.
Take the enemy's strength from him by stealing away his
supplies.

Your customers cannot afford expensive shipping and transportation.
Selling to distant customers is costly.
Buying raw materials that are popular is also expensive.
High initial costs make it difficult to satisfy customers.
The on-going overhead costs of running a business drain you.
These costs can easily consume all your profits.
Even though you are making sales, your business produces nothing.

Too little profit destroys most new businesses.
Eighty percent fail within the first two years.
You spend the money that you've saved.
When the business fails, your investment is lost.
Your inventory becomes worthless.
Your spending in sales and advertising is wasted.
Your equipment and offices are abandoned.
Failure will consume most of what you've accumulated.

Because of the risks, you must be certain to make profitable sales.

Take a dollar in profits.
It is worth twenty dollars of potential.
Sell your most profitable products.
They are worth twenty products that make nothing.

You must be productive and indispensable.
You must generate more value in the business than your expenses consume.

Fight for the enemy's supply wagons.
Capture their supplies by using overwhelming force.
Reward the first who capture them.
Then change their banners and flags.
Mix them in with your own to increase your supply line.
Keep your soldiers strong by providing for them.
This is what it means to beat the enemy while you grow more powerful.

Make victory in war pay for itself.
Avoid expensive, long campaigns.
The military commander's knowledge is the key.
It determines if the civilian officials can govern.
It determines if the nation's households are peaceful or a danger to the state.

Steal profitable ideas from competitors.
Concentrate your efforts on the most profitable customers.
Reward your early customers for choosing you.
Advertise and promote your uniqueness.
Remix profitable products to invent a new type of business.
Keep your business strong by making it profitable.
This is what it means to beat competitors while growing stronger.

Make your new business pay for itself.
Avoid expensive, slow start-ups.
Knowledge of your industry is the key.
It determines your ability to control your business.
It decides whether or not your business is valuable or dangerous to your future.

PLANNING AN ATTACK

Everyone relies on the arts of war.
A united nation is strong.
A divided nation is weak.
A united army is strong.
A divided army is weak.
A united force is strong.
A divided force is weak.
United men are strong.
Divided men are weak.
A united unit is strong.
A divided unit is weak.

Unity works because it enables you to win every battle you fight.
Still, this is the foolish goal of a weak leader.
Avoid battle and make the enemy's men surrender.
This is the right goal for a superior leader.

DEVELOPING A FOCUS

Everyone depends on the rules of competition.
A focused business is successful.
An unfocused business isn't.
A united team is successful.
A divided team isn't.
A concentrated effort is successful.
A divided effort isn't.
Well defined market targets make you successful.
A general group of customers doesn't.
Clear-cut goals make you successful.
Confused goals don't.

The more focused you are, the easier it will be to solve problems.
Still, solving problems alone doesn't build a solid business.
Avoid problems and satisfy your customers.
This is right goal for a successful business.

21

The best policy is to attack while the enemy is still planning.
The next best is to disrupt alliances.
The next best is to attack the opposing army.
The worst is to attack the enemy's cities.

This is what happens when you attack a city.
You can attempt it, but you can't finish it.
First you must make siege engines.
You need the right equipment and machinery.
You use three months and still cannot win.
Then, you try to encircle the area.
You use three more months without making progress.
The commander still doesn't win and this angers him.
He then tries to swarm the city.
This kills a third of his officers and men.
He still isn't able to draw the enemy out of the city.
This attack is a disaster.

Make good use of war.
Make the enemy's troops surrender.
You can do this fighting only minor battles.
You can draw their men out of their cities.
You can do it with small attacks.
You can destroy the men of a nation.
You must keep your campaign short.

It's best to start a business that others are still planning.
The next best is to join existing partnerships.
The next best is to improve an existing business.
The worst is competing against an established business.

What happens when you attack a good business?
You can try to duplicate their system, but you won't do it.
First, you must copy their organization.
You need all their equipment and systems.
Systems take time to work, and you still don't succeed.
Then, you try to do everything that they do.
After spreading yourself too thin, you don't make money.
You will get frustrated and angry.
You then try advertising to win their customers.
This costs you more money.
You are still unable to make a dent in an existing business.
This type of business start-up is a disaster.

Make good progress starting a business.
Let customers come to you.
You do this by starting small.
Win customers away from other businesses.
You do it by picking a niche in which to compete.
You must protect your resources.
You must make profits quickly.

You must use total war, fighting with everything you have.
Never stop fighting when at war.
You can gain complete advantage.
To do this, you must plan your strategy of attack.

The rules for making war are:
If you outnumber the enemy ten to one, surround them.
If you outnumber them five to one, attack them.
If you outnumber them two to one, divide them.
If you are equal, then find an advantageous battle.
If you are fewer, defend against them.
If you are much weaker, evade them.

Small forces are not powerful.
However, large forces cannot catch them.

You must master command.
The nation must support you.

Supporting the military makes the nation powerful.
Not supporting the military makes the nation weak.

Politicians create problems for the military in three different
ways.
Ignorant of the army's inability to advance, they order an
advance.
Ignorant of the army's inability to withdraw, they order a
withdrawal.
We call this tying up the army.
Politicians don't understand the army's business.
Still, they think they can run an army.
This confuses the army's officers.

24

You must be totally committed to succeeding at business.
Work every day to build your customer base.
You can find good opportunities.
To do this, you must develop a concept for marketing.

The rules for promoting a business are these:
If you are ten time bigger than competitors, advertise.
If you are five times bigger, contact the customer.
If you are twice as big, divide the market.
If you are the same size, specialize.
If you are smaller, defend a small segment.
If you are much smaller, find a tiny niche.

Small companies are not powerful.
However, large companies cannot compete in niches.

$\longmapsto$

You must be able to manage your finances.
Your finances must support you.

Supporting a business will make you financially strong.
Not supporting a business will make you financially weak.

Bad management creates financial problems for a business
in three ways.
Regardless of business needs, people spend money freely
when they have it.
Regardless of business needs, people take out money
because they want it.
We call this hamstringing the business.
Poor managers don't understand the needs of the business.
They still think they can spend what they want.
This only throws the business into chaos.

Politicians don't know the army's chain of command.
They give the army too much freedom.
This will create distrust among the army's officers.

The entire army becomes confused and distrusting.
This invites invasion from many different rivals.
We say correctly that disorder in an army kills victory.

You must know five things to win:
Victory comes from knowing when to attack and when to
avoid battle.
Victory comes from correctly using large and small forces.
Victory comes from everyone sharing the same goals.
Victory comes from finding opportunities in problems.
Victory comes from having a capable commander and the
government leaving him alone.
You must know these five things.
You then know the theory of victory.

We say:
"Know yourself and know your enemy.
You will be safe in every battle.
You may know yourself but not know the enemy.
You will then lose one battle for every one you win.
You may not know yourself or the enemy.
You will then lose every battle."

Bad managers misunderstand financial priorities.
They spend too freely.
This creates uncertainty in the business's future.

All businesses are at first financially unstable.
This invites future cash shortages.
A lack of priorities destroys your chances of success.

You must know five things to build a business
Success comes from knowing what needs doing and what
can be left undone.
Success comes from performing small and large tasks.
Success comes from understanding your customers' needs.
Success comes from turning problems into opportunities.
Success comes from learning to manage and avoiding
financial problems.
You must know these five things.
You then know the concepts of building a business.

Experience says this:
Know your capabilities and your competitors.
If you do, you will be safe competing.
You may know your capabilities but not your competitors.
Then, for every success, you will have a setback.
If you know neither your capabilities nor your competitors.
Then, you will have nothing but setbacks.

POSITIONING

Learn from the history of successful battles.
Your first actions should deny victory to the enemy.
You pay attention to your enemy to find the way to win.
You alone can deny victory to the enemy.
Only your enemy can allow you to win.

You must fight well.
You can prevent the enemy's victory.
You cannot win unless the enemy enables your victory.

We say:
You see the opportunity for victory; you don't create it.

You are sometimes unable to win.
You must then defend.
You will eventually be able to win.
You must then attack.
Defend when you have insufficient strength to win.
Attack when you have more strength than you need to win.

MARKETING

Learn from the history of successful businesses.
First, you must generate revenues.
You pay attention to the marketplace to find opportunities.
You can only keep your customers from competitors.
Competitors leave the market opening for you to succeed.

You must execute well.
You can prevent losing existing customers.
You cannot win new ones unless there is a market need.

It is said:
You must discover your market niche; you do not create it.

You cannot always find a new market.
You must then concentrate on your existing customers.
You will eventually discover a better market.
Then you must go after new customers.
Avoid markets that are too large for you to dominate.
Go after markets that are small enough for you to dominate.

You must defend yourself well.
Save your forces and dig in.
You must attack well.
Move your forces when you have a clear advantage.

You must protect your forces until you can completely
triumph.

Some may see how to win.
However, they cannot position their forces where they must.
This demonstrates limited ability.

Some can struggle to a victory and the whole world may
praise their winning.
This also demonstrates a limited ability.

Win as easily as picking up a fallen hair.
Don't use all of your forces.
See the time to move.
Don't try to find something clever.
Hear the clap of thunder.
Don't try to hear something subtle.

Learn from the history of successful battles.
Victory goes to those who make winning easy.
A good battle is one that you will obviously win.
It doesn't take intelligence to win a reputation.
It doesn't take courage to achieve success.

You must defend existing customers well.
Save your resources and dig in.
You must campaign for new customers well.
Go after a new market when you have a clear opportunity.

You must conserve your marketing resources until you see
a market you can win.

You may see new customers that you would like.
Yet you don't see how to contact those customers.
This shows limited ability.

You may win customers by spending a lot of money on
marketing.
This also shows limited ability.

Move into new markets effortlessly.
Avoid risking your current customers.
Wait for the time to move.
Don't try to be too clever.
Learning about opportunities is easy if you listen.
Don't imagine opportunities where you want them.

Learn from the history of successful businesses.
Success goes to those who make work easy.
A good customer is one who is inexpensive to win.
It doesn't take a genius to get known in a market.
Don't take chances when it comes to success.

You must win your battles without effort.
Avoid difficult struggles.
Fight when your position must win.
You always win by preventing your defeat.

You must engage only in winning battles.
Position yourself where you cannot lose.
Never waste an opportunity to defeat your enemy.

You win a war by first assuring yourself of victory.
Only afterward do you look for a fight.
Outmaneuver the enemy before the battle and then fight to
win.

You must make good use of war.
Study military philosophy and the art of defense.
You can control your victory or defeat.

This is the art of war.
1. Discuss the distances.
2. Discuss your numbers.
3. Discuss your calculations.
4. Discuss your decisions.
5. Discuss victory.
The ground determines the distance.
The distance determines your numbers.
Your numbers determine your calculations.
Your calculations determine your decisions.
Your decisions determine your victory.

You want to win a new business without effort.
Avoid highly competitive situations.
Do business that you know you can do well.
You succeed if you avoid impossible jobs.

You must engage only in successful projects.
Sell to markets that are easy to satisfy.
Never pass by an opportunity to win customers.

Build a good business by first finding the right customers.
Only then do you worry about the work.
Find the right customers for your business and then work to satisfy them.

§—⚓

You must build your business carefully.
Study competitive methods and protect your market.
You alone determine your success or failure.

The art of starting a business is this:
1. An analysis of the obstacles
2. An analysis of your resources
3. An analysis of profit potential
4. An analysis of your market commitment
5. An analysis of your success
The marketplace determine the obstacles.
Those obstacles determine the resources required.
The resources required determine the profit potential.
The profit potential determines your market commitment.
Your market commitment determines your success.

Creating a winning war is like balancing a coin of gold against
a coin of silver.
Creating a losing war is like balancing coin of a silver against
a coin of gold.

Winning a battle is always a matter of people.
You pour them into battle like a flood of water pouring into a
deep gorge.
This is a matter of positioning.

Creating a successful business is a matter of wooing the best customers over second-rate ones.
Business failure comes from wooing all customers instead of looking for the best ones.

Success in business is always a matter of people.
You want to identify customers that find your business irresistible.
This depends on your marketing.

MOMENTUM

You control a large army as you control a few men.
You just divide their ranks correctly.
You fight a large army the same as you fight a small one.
You only need the right position and communication.
You may meet a large enemy army.
You must be able to encounter the enemy without being
defeated.
You must correctly use both surprise and direct action.
Your army's position must increase your strength.
Troops flanking an enemy can smash them like eggs.
You must correctly use both strength and weakness.

It is the same in all battles.
You use a direct approach to engage the enemy.
You use surprise to win.

You must use surprise for a successful invasion.
Surprise is as infinite as the weather and land.
Surprise is as inexhaustible as the flow of a river.

36

CONTINUAL IMPROVEMENT

You control a large business the same as a small one.
You need only to build the right organization.
You win large markets the same way you win small ones.
You need the right brand identity and marketing.
You may meet larger competitors.
You can compete against them, and you should never lose
to them.
You need to use creative and standard business methods.
Together, they increase your momentum in the market.
Build your business in ways that surprise competitors.
You must understand both your strengths and weaknesses.

It is the same in all businesses.
You use established practices to start the business.
You use innovation to beat the competition.

Use innovation to grow your business.
There are an infinite number of business improvements.
Innovation harnesses the flow of change in business.

You can be stopped and yet recover the initiative.
You must use your days and months correctly.

If you are defeated, you can recover.
You must use the four seasons correctly.

There are only a few notes in the scale.
Yet, you can always rearrange them.
You can never hear every song of victory.

'There are only a few basic colors.
Yet, you can always mix them.
You can never see all the shades of victory.

There are only a few flavors.
Yet, you can always blend them.
You can never taste all the flavors of victory.

You fight with momentum.
There are only a few types of surprises and direct actions.
Yet, you can always vary the ones you use.
There is no limit to the ways you can win.

Surprise and direct action give birth to each other.
They proceed from each other in an endless cycle.
You can not exhaust all their possible combinations!

Today's difficulties are the seeds of tomorrow's success.
Use time to continually improve your operation.

You can make mistakes and still move forward.
It takes time to get innovations working.

There are only a few basic messages for selling products.
But you can rearrange messages in creative ways.
You can always inspire customers' fresh interest.

There are only a few basic components to a product.
But you can mix them together in different ways.
You can always invent new types of product.

There are only a few basic business processes.
But you can combine the steps in new ways.
You can always find a better way to get the work done.

You build business with continual improvement.
Improvement is using innovation with proven practices.
You can combine both to make your business unique.
There are no limits to the ways you can create profits.

Innovation and proven practices are mutually dependent.
Standards inspire creativity, which inspires new standards.
Using both, you can continually improve your business.

Surging water flows together rapidly.
Its pressure washes away boulders.
This is momentum.

A hawk suddenly strikes a bird.
Its contact alone kills the prey.
This is timing.

You must fight only winning battles.
Your momentum must be overwhelming.
Your timing must be exact.

Your momentum is like the tension of a bent crossbow.
Your timing is like the pulling of a trigger.

War is complicated and confused.
Battle is chaotic.
Nevertheless, you must not allow chaos.

War is sloppy and messy.
Positions turn around.
Nevertheless, you must never be defeated.

Chaos gives birth to control.
Fear gives birth to courage.
Weakness gives birth to strength.

You must control chaos.
This depends on your planning.
Your men must brave their fears.
This depends on their momentum.

Small changes should come together quickly.
These changes can wash away big problems.
This is continual improvement.

A customer's decision takes place in an instant.
Sales contact alone wins the business.
This is quickness.

You must invest only in profitable business.
Your improvements must make you superior.
Your quickness must make you profitable.

Your improvements increase the quality of your business.
Your quickness generates the profits you need.

Commerce is always complicated and confused.
Competition is unpredictable.
Still, you must create orderly systems.

Business is never neat and tidy.
Situations are always changing.
Nevertheless, you must never lose customers.

The confusion of commerce demands organization.
The uncertainty of business demands certainty.
The needs of customers require your ability.

You must control what is disorganized.
This depends on your business analysis.
Your business must overcome its problems.
This depends on continual improvement.

41

You have strengths and weaknesses.
These come from your position.

You must force the enemy to move to your advantage.
Use your position.
The enemy must follow you.
Surrender a position.
The enemy must take it.
You can offer an advantage to move him.
You can use your men to move him.
You use your strength to hold him.

You want a successful battle.
To do this, you must seek momentum.
Do not just demand a good fight from your people.
You must pick good people and then give them momentum.

You must create momentum.
You create it with your men during battle.
This is comparable to rolling trees and stones.
Trees and stones roll because of their shape and weight.
Offer men safety and they will stay calm.
Endanger them and they will act.
Give them a place and they will hold.
Round them up and they will march.

You make your men powerful in battle with momentum.
This is just like rolling round stones down over a high, steep
cliff.
Use your momentum.

You have both strengths and weaknesses.
They arise from your marketing.

You must encourage customers to create opportunities.
Use your marketing.
Customers must listen to you.
Offer great value.
The customer must take it.
You can offer benefits to interest customers.
You can use your activities to convince them.
You use your efficiency to keep them.

You want to win profitable business.
You do this by looking to continually improve.
Do not just ask your people to work harder.
Find a method to improve the way they work.

You must generate improvements.
You do this with your employees as you work.
Business activities should flow together easily.
Processes should come together with minimal effort.
Make work easy and employees will work comfortably.
Make mistakes visible and employees will avoid them.
Give them a goal and they will reach it.
Get them working together and they will move forward.

You make yourself powerful in a business by improvement.
The work gets done almost automatically when everything
is organized.
Use continual improvement.

WEAKNESS AND STRENGTH

Always arrive first to the empty battlefield to await the
enemy at your leisure.
If you are late and hurry to the battlefield, fighting is more
difficult.

You want a successful battle.
Move your men, but not into opposing forces.

You can make the enemy come to you.
Offer him an advantage.
You can make the enemy avoid coming to you.
Threaten him with danger.

When the enemy is fresh, you can tire him.
When he is well fed, you can starve him.
When he is relaxed, you can move him.

Problems and Solutions

You want the advantage of solving problems before the customer encounters them.
If you let problems affect customers, starting a business is difficult.

You want a profitable business.
Change your operations, but do not create problems.

You can make customers come to you.
Entice them with unique offerings.
You can stop the competition from copying you.
Pick a product that is dangerous for them.

If trust is a problem, make customers comfortable.
If satisfaction is a problem, address customers' needs.
If indifference is a problem, get customers excited.

Leave any place without haste.
Hurry to where you are not expected.
You can easily march hundreds of miles without tiring.
To do so, travel through areas that are deserted.
You must take whatever you attack.
Attack when there is no defense.
You must have walls to defend.
Defend where it is impossible to attack.

Be skilled in attacking.
Give the enemy no idea of where to defend.

Be skillful in your defense.
Give the enemy no idea of where to attack.

Be subtle! Be subtle!
Arrive without any clear formation.
Quietly! Quietly!
Arrive without a sound.
You must use all your skill to control the enemy's decisions.

Advance to where they can't defend.
Charge through their openings.
Withdraw where the enemy cannot chase you.
Move quickly so that they cannot catch you.

Abandon any established business gradually.
Win new customers before competitors do.
You can change a business dramatically without difficulty.
To do so, find problems that no one else addresses.
You can solve the problems that you tackle.
Work where needs are unsatisfied.
Keep customers that you have won.
Leave no needs for your competitors to satisfy.

Be skilled in providing solutions.
Find problems that others have left unresolved.

Be skilled in avoiding problems.
Provide solutions before others can address them.

Be sensitive to customers' needs.
Go to them without selling your product.
Keep quiet about what you offer.
Go to them willing to listen.
Use your skills to shape their buying decisions.

Propose solutions where they have problems.
Directly address their complaints.
Offer solutions that competitors cannot equal.
Move quickly so that competitors cannot copy you.

I always pick my own battles.
The enemy can hide behind high walls and deep trenches.
I do not try to win by fighting him directly.
Instead, I attack a place that he must rescue.
I avoid the battles that I don't want.
I can divide the ground and yet defend it.
I don't give the enemy anything to win.
Divert him from coming to where you defend.

I make their men take a position while I take none.
I then focus my forces where the enemy divides his forces.
Where I focus, I unite my forces.
When the enemy divides, he creates many small groups.
I want my large group to attack one of his small ones.
Then I have many men where the enemy has but a few.
My large force can overwhelm his small one.
I then go on to the next small enemy group.
I will take them one at a time.

We must keep the place that we've chosen as a battleground
a secret.
The enemy must not know.
Force the enemy to prepare his defense in many places.
I want the enemy to defend many places.
Then I can choose where to fight.
His forces will be weak there.

Pick customer problems that you can best address.
Your competitors may be able to defend their businesses.
You cannot beat competitors by going after them directly.
Instead, find problems that they have overlooked.
Avoid business that you do not want.
You can turn down business and still win customers.
Do not let competitors win the jobs that you want.
Specialize to a degree that they cannot compete with you.

8—⊸

Know what competitors do well before starting a business.
Focus your business on gaps in competing businesses.
When you focus, you concentrate your energies.
Where competitors divide their attention, they create needs.
You must focus your efforts on unmet needs.
You can put more resources into your specialty.
You can easily do a better job there than competitors can.
You can then move on to the next group of competitors.
Tackle customer problems one at a time.

8—⊸

You must keep your business specialty a secret from your
competitors.
You want ignorant competitors.
Encourage competitors to sell a wide variety of products.
They must spread themselves too thin.
You can then choose the specialty that you want.
Their offering will be weak there.

If he reinforces his front lines, he depletes his rear.
If he reinforces his rear, he depletes his front.
If he reinforces his right, he depletes his left.
If he reinforces his left, he depletes his right.
Without knowing the place of attack, he cannot prepare.
Without a place, he will be weak everywhere.

The enemy has weak points.
Prepare your men against them.
He has strong points.
Make his men prepare themselves against you.

You must know the battle ground.
You must know the time of battle.
You can then travel a thousand miles and still win the battle.

The enemy should not know the battleground.
He shouldn't know the time of battle.
His left will be unable to support his right.
His right will be unable to support his left.
His front lines will be unable to support his rear.
His rear will be unable to support his front.
His support is distant even if it is only ten miles away.
What unknown place can be close?

We control the balance of forces.
The enemy may have many men but they are superfluous.
How can they help him to victory?

If competitors specialize in price, they sacrifice quality.
If they specialize in quality, they are vulnerable in price.
If they specialize in speed, they lack accuracy.
If they specialize in accuracy, they lose on speed.
Ignorant of your specialty, they leave an opening for you.
If they attempt everything, they leave openings everywhere.

All customers have needs.
Create your business to address those needs.
Competitors offer specific solutions.
They cannot satisfy every type of customer.

You must understand the problem you are solving.
You must know how important it is.
Even if a solution is expensive, you must still make money.

Your competitors must not understand the problem.
They shouldn't know how to solve it.
If competitors work globally, you focus locally.
If they offer popular products, you can offer unique ones.
If they deal in large volumes, you can offer small ones.
If they use standard terms, you can create special ones.
They will continually overlook your customer.
What unknown business is easy?

You control how much competition you have.
Competitors may be bigger, but your business is unique.
How can their size hurt you?

We say:
You must let victory happen.

The enemy may have many men.
You can still control him without a fight.

When you form your strategy, know the strengths and
weaknesses of your plan.
When you execute, know how to manage both action and
inaction.
When you take a position, know the deadly and the winning
grounds.
When you battle, know when you have too many or too few
men.

Use your position as your war's centerpiece.
Arrive at the battle without a formation.
Don't take a position.
Then even the best spies can't report it.
Even the wisest general cannot plan to counter you.
Take a position where you can triumph using superior
numbers.
Keep the enemy's forces ignorant.
Their troops will learn of my location when my position will
win.
They must not know how our location gives us a winning
position.
Make the battle one from which they cannot recover.
You must always adjust your position to their position.

We teach this:
You must let your business succeed.

Competitors may be much bigger than you are.
You can still control them by avoiding comparisons.

When you create a business plan, know its strengths and weaknesses.
When you start your business, know what needs to be done and what does not.
When you pick customers, know which people are satisfied and which people have needs.
When you compete, know when you have the advantage and when you are overmatched.

Use your unique offerings to draw special customers.
Do not go into business copying what others offer.
Do not duplicate competitors.
Then most jaded customers cannot discount you.
The toughest competitors will not know how to beat you.
Only go after customers you can satisfy better than anyone else.
Work where your competitors are ignorant.
Competitors should only learn of your business when you win sales.
Competitors should not know how to copy what you are selling.
Make sure that they cannot win customers back from you.
If they try to better you, copy any moves they make.

Manage your military position like water.
Water takes every shape.
It avoids the high and moves to the low.
Your war can take any shape.
It must avoid the strong and strike the weak.
Water follows the shape of the land that directs its flow.
Your forces follow the enemy who determines how you win.

Make war without a standard approach.
Water has no consistent shape.
If you follow the enemy's shifts and changes, you can always win.
We call this shadowing.

Fight five different campaigns without a firm rule for victory.
Use all four seasons without a consistent position.
Your timing must be sudden.
A few weeks determine your failure or success.

You must remain fluid in starting your business.
Your business can work in many different ways.
You start where you can make money and then expand.
Your business can take any shape.
You must avoid competitors and address people's needs.
Sales should shape your business and set its direction.
You discover customers and let them guide your actions.

You must avoid rigid business plans.
Good ideas have no consistent shape.
Understand the change in customer thinking, and you will succeed.
This is called shadowing.

Different businesses call for different methods to succeed.
Different times need flexibility in your business approach.
You must always act quickly.
A moment may determine your success or failure.

ARMED CONFLICT

Everyone uses the arts of war.
You accept orders from the government.
Then you assemble your army.
You organize your men and build camps.
You must avoid disasters from armed conflict.

Seeking armed conflict can be disastrous.
Because of this, a detour can be the shortest path.
Because of this, problems can become opportunities.

Use an indirect route as your highway.
Use the search for advantage to guide you.
When you fall behind, you must catch up.
When you get ahead, you must wait.
You must know the detour that most directly accomplishes
your plan.

Undertake armed conflict when you have an advantage.
Seeking armed conflict for its own sake is dangerous.

Making Sales

Everyone uses their business sense.
You get your inspiration from the marketplace.
You put together your resources.
You set up your operation and open for business.
You must then avoid mistakes in sales contact.

Selling is uncomfortable for everyone.
You cannot plan the path a sale will take.
You must expect problems and turn them into opportunities.

You must plan to work hard at making sales.
You must plan to entice customers with benefits.
When you lose a sale, you must know how to make it up.
When you get ahead of the customer, you must slow down.
You must know how to plan for both objection and
agreement.

You alone can make the sales contact successful.
All customer contact is inherently difficult.

You can build up an army to fight for an advantage.
Then you won't catch the enemy.
You can force your army to go fight for an advantage.
Then you abandon your heavy supply wagons.

You keep only your armor and hurry straight after the enemy.
You avoid stopping day or night.
You use many roads at the same time.
You go hundreds of miles to fight for an advantage.
Then the enemy catches your commanders and your army.
Your strong soldiers get there first.
Your weaker soldiers follow behind.
Using this approach, only one in ten will arrive.
You can try to go fifty miles to fight for an advantage.
Then your commanders and army will stumble.
Using this method, only half of your soldiers will make it.
You can try to go thirty miles to fight for an advantage.
Then only two out of three get there.

If you make your army travel without good supply lines, they
will die.
Without supplies and food, your army will die.
If you don't save the harvest, your army will die.

You can argue with people about why they should buy.
You will then lose customers.
You can rush through the sale extolling your virtues.
You then fail to learn about the customer.

You can try to rush the customer into making a decision.
You can pressure him or her to buy.
You can try many different arguments at the same time.
You can spend all your time praising your product.
The customer can still reject your product and approach.
You think you are winning the sale at first.
Over time the customer will ignore you.
Only a small fraction of your effort is useful.
You can try less pressure in the sales process.
You will still lose sales that you should have made.
You waste half your efforts.
You can press for sales that are almost closed.
You may win two out of three.

You can try to shortcut the process of making a sale, but it
will cost you sales.
Without the proper information, you can not sell.
Without the proper groundwork, you can not sell.

Do not let any of your potential enemies know of what you are planning.
You must stay with the enemy.
You must know the lay of the land.
You must know where the obstructions are.
You must know where the marshes are.
If you don't, you cannot move the army.
You must use local guides.
If you don't, you can't take advantage of the terrain.

You make war using a deceptive position.
If you use deception, then you can move.
Using deception, you can upset the enemy and change the situation.
You must move as quickly as the wind.
You must rise like the forest.
You must invade and plunder like fire.
You must stay as motionless as a mountain.
You must be as mysterious as the fog.
You must strike like sounding thunder.

Divide your troops to plunder the villages.
When on open ground, dividing is an advantage.
Don't worry about organization, just move.
Be the first to find a new route that leads directly to a winning plan.
This is the how you are successful at armed conflict.

Instead, you must initially keep quiet about what you are selling.
You must meet with people and talk with them.
You must know the customers' needs.
You must know where their problems are.
You must avoid bogging down in technicalities.
You must be knowledgeable to make the sale.
You must rely on your understanding of customers.
You must take advantage of the customers' thinking.

You must disguise your desire to make a sale.
If the customer doesn't fight you, you can make progress.
You uncover their problems, understand them, and use the situation.
To make sales, you must think on your feet.
You must be forthright and determined
You must be aggressive and hungry.
You must be quiet and patient.
You must keep your goals to yourself.
You must be brave enough to ask for the business.

When making sales, prioritize your activities.
When a sales opportunity comes, come to an agreement.
Don't think about it, just act.
Find better ways to help customers find happiness in their lives.
This is the how you are successful at making sales.

Military experience says:
"You can speak, but you will not be heard.
You must use gongs and drums.
You cannot really see your forces just by looking.
You must use banners and flags."

You must master gongs, drums, banners and flags.
Place people as a single unit where they can all see and hear.
You must unite them as one.
Then, the brave cannot advance alone.
The fearful cannot withdraw alone.
You must force them to act as a group.

In night battles, you must use numerous fires and drums.
In day battles, you must use many banners and flags.
You must position your people to control what they see and
hear.

You control your army by controlling its emotions.
As a general, you must be able to control emotions.

In the morning, a person's energy is high.
During the day, it fades.
By evening, a person's thoughts turn to home.
You must use your troops wisely.
Avoid the enemy's high spirits.
Strike when they are lazy and want to go home.
This is how you master energy.

Experience in sales teaches us:
"Words alone are not enough.
Use pictures and charts.
Demonstrating is not enough.
Use showmanship and magic."

Use pictures, props, and showmanship to get people's
attention.
Tie your sales presentation together.
Don't offer innovative concepts alone.
Tie them together with comfortable, familiar ideas.
Every word must amplify a single, clear message.

When unknown, you must create excitement and interest.
If you are better known, you still must keep it interesting.
You must offer a product that everyone can understand and
appreciate.

8—⚷

You must get your customer's attention.
To make sales, you must use emotion.

At first, customer resistance is high.
Over time, it fades.
By the end, they want to go home.
You must use your time wisely.
Avoid customer resistance.
Close when resistance fades and they want to go home.
This is how you master energy.

Use discipline to await the chaos of battle.
Keep relaxed to await a crisis.
This is how you master emotion.

Stay close to home to await a distant enemy.
Stay comfortable to await the weary enemy.
Stay well fed to await the hungry enemy.
This is how you master power.

Don't entice the enemy when their ranks are orderly.
You must not attack when their formations are solid
This is how you master adaptation.
You must follow these military rules.
Do not take a position facing the high ground.
Do not oppose those with their backs to wall.
Do not follow those who pretend to flee.
Do not attack the enemy's strongest men.
Do not swallow the enemy's bait.
Do not block an army that is heading home.
Leave an escape outlet for a surrounded army.
Do not press a desperate foe.
This is the art of war.

Keep organized when the customer is confused.
Stay quiet while the customer blows off steam.
This is how you master your emotions.

Stick to your point and wait for others to respond.
Stay friendly as you wear down the customer's resistance.
You will be successful if you serve the needs of others.
This is how you master persuasion.

Do not create organized resistance.
Do not attack firmly held beliefs.
This is how you master adapting.
You must follow these rules for selling.
Do not take a position against strong feelings.
Do not fight an argument based on a lack of alternatives.
Do not accept those who only pretend to agree.
Do not attack the toughest arguments against you.
Do not believe everything the customer tells you.
Do not argue with a customer who agrees with you.
Give the customer an agreeable alternative.
Do not press the customer too hard for a decision.
These are the rules of selling.

ADAPTABILITY

Everyone uses the arts of war.
As a general, you get your orders from the government.
You gather your troops.
On dangerous ground, you must not camp.
Where the roads intersect, you must join your allies.
When an area is cut off, you must not delay in it.
When you are surrounded, you must scheme.
In a life-or-death situation, you must fight.
There are roads that you must not take.
There are armies that you must not fight.
There are strongholds that you must not attack.
There are positions that you must not defend.
There are government commands that must not be obeyed.

Military leaders must be experts in knowing how to adapt to
win.
This will teach you the use of war.

Adjusting to the Situation

Everyone uses their business sense.
You get your inspiration from the marketplace.
You put together your resources.
When business is slow, you must not waste your time.
When you need help, you must make partners.
When customers reject you, you must not give up.
When you are outmaneuvered, you must get creative.
When you are in a do-or-die situation, you must win.
There are products and services you should not sell.
There are customers that you don't want.
There are competitors that you cannot challenge.
There are mistakes that you must not defend.
There are times to ignore standard operating procedures.

You must become an expert at knowing how to adapt to win
a sale.
Adapting to the situation is the key to business success.

Some commanders are not good at making adjustments to
find an advantage.
They can know the shape of the terrain.
Still, they can not find an advantageous position.

Some military commanders do not know how to adjust their
methods.
They can find an advantageous position.
Still, they can not use their men effectively.

You must be creative in your planning.
You must adapt to your opportunities and weaknesses.
You can use a variety of approaches and still have a
consistent result.
You must adjust to a variety of problems and consistently
solve them.

You can deter your potential enemy by using his weaknesses
against him.
You can keep your enemy's army busy by giving it work to do.
You can rush your enemy by offering him an advantageous
position.

Some business people are unable to change their offering to fit a given situation.
They might know what the customer desires.
Still, they cannot develop a product that customers want.

Some business people do not know how to adjust their methods.
They know what their customers want.
Still, they are unable to change so they can offer it.

You must be inventive in offering your products.
There are strengths and weaknesses in every offering.
You can offer different products at different times and still consistently win sales.
Every situation offers unique problems, but you can always find a good solution.

Customers choose a product because they see shortcomings in competing products.
Engage customers by interesting them in your products.
You can improve the pace of sales by giving customers a reason to buy now.

You must make use of war.
Do not trust that the enemy isn't coming.
Trust on your readiness to meet him.
Do not trust that the enemy won't attack.
We must rely only on our ability to pick a place that the
enemy can't attack.

You can exploit five different faults in a leader.
If he is willing to die, you can kill him.
If he wants to survive, you can capture him.
He may have a quick temper.
You can then provoke him with insults.
If he has a delicate sense of honor, you can disgrace him.
If he loves his people, you can create problems for him.
In every situation, look for these five weaknesses.
They are common faults in commanders.
They always lead to military disaster.

To overturn an army, you must kill its general.
To do this, you must use these five weaknesses.
You must always look for them.

You must use your resources carefully.

Do not expect to win any sale easily.

Instead, be ready to meet resistance.

Do not trust that competitors won't attack your product.

Instead, position your product so that others can't easily attack it.

People starting a business can have five character flaws.

If they are willing to lose a sale, they will lose it.

If they lack courage, they will give products away.

If they have a quick temper, they will be provoked.

If they are sensitive to rejection, they can't ask for the sale.

If they are sensitive to criticism, they ignore problems.

If they love their methods, they won't improve them.

In every situation, look for these five weaknesses.

They are common failures of new business owners.

They can lead you to disaster in starting your business.

These weaknesses can destroy you and your business.

You must know how to exploit them in others.

You must always be aware of them.

Armed March

Everyone moving their army must adjust to the enemy.

Keep out of the mountains and in the valleys.
Position yourself on the heights facing the sun.
To win your battles, never attack uphill.
This is how you position your army in the mountains.

When water blocks you, keep far away from it.
Let the enemy cross the river and wait for him.
Do not meet him in midstream.
Wait for him to get half his forces across and then take
advantage of the situation.

You need to be able to fight.
You can't do that if you are in the water when you meet an
attack.
Position yourself upstream, facing the sun.
Never face against the current.
Always position your army upstream when near the water.

MAKING PROGRESS

In every business, you must serve the customer.

Avoid costly commitments and make small improvements.
Keep your business visible and accessible.
To tackle problems, never throw money at them.
This is how to make progress in expensive situations.

When a new technology will limit you, avoid it.
Let your competitors invest in it and use time against them.
Don't compete for the latest technology.
Wait until a technology is well proven and then take
advantage of falling prices.

You need to be productive.
You can't if you are wrestling with technology instead of
serving your customers.
Use technology to make your processes visible.
Never fight against technological trends.
Leverage the trends when implementing a technology.

You may have to move across marshes.
Move through them quickly without stopping.
You may meet the enemy in the middle of a marsh.
You must keep on the water grasses.
Keep your back to a clump of trees.
This is how you position your army in a marsh.

On a level plateau, take a position that you can change.
Keep the higher ground on your right and to the rear.
Keep the danger in front of you and safety behind.
This is how you position yourself on a level plateau.

You can find an advantage in all four of these situations.
Learn from the great emperor who used positioning to
conquer his four rivals.

Armies are stronger on high ground and weaker on low.
They are better camping on sunny, southern hillsides than on
the shady, northern ones.
Provide for your army's health and place it well.
Your army will be free from disease.
Done correctly, this means victory.

You must sometimes defend on a hill or riverbank.
You must keep on the south side in the sun.
Keep the uphill slope at your right rear.

This will give the advantage to your army.
It will always give you a position of strength.

You may have to implement short-term solutions.
Use them briefly and never leave them in place.
You will have problems with short-term solutions.
When you do, keep what is working well.
Work toward a solid, long-term resolution.
This is how you make progress in the short-term.

When conditions are stable, identify what can be improved.
Invest in advertising and business infrastructure.
Make problems visible and protect what works.
This is how to make progress in stable situations.

You can make progress in any situation.
Learn from successful owners who have continually
improved their business.

Businesses are stronger with cash and weaker without it.
You are better with solid, cash reserves than with forecasted
budget surpluses.
Keep your business healthy by keeping it cash-rich.
Your organization will be free from the pressures of debt.
Do this correctly, and you will be successful.

Sometimes you must borrow money.
Keep the loan small and keep track of it.
Use it to build your business.

This will create opportunities for your business.
Cash always gives you a position of strength.

Stop the march when the rain swells the river into rapids.
You may want to ford the river.
Wait until it subsides.

All regions have dead-ends such as waterfalls.
There are deep lakes.
There are high cliffs.
There are dense jungles.
There are thick quagmires.
There are steep crevasses.
Get away from all these quickly.
Do not get close to them.
Keep them at a distance.
Maneuver the enemy close to them.
Position yourself facing these dangers.
Push the enemy back into them.

Danger can hide on your army's flank.
There are reservoirs and lakes.
There are reeds and thickets.
There are forests of trees.
Their dense vegetation provides a hiding place.
You must cautiously search through them.
They can always hide an ambush.

Stop making changes when technology is changing.
You may want to use an evolving technology.
Wait until it stabilizes.

All businesses have limits that restrict what can be done.
There are resource limitations.
There are cost limitations.
There are information limitations.
There are legal limitations.
There are span of control limitations.
Always avoid these limitations.
Do not get close to your business's limits.
Leave yourself plenty of room.
You want to limit only your problems.
Keep your eye on your problems.
Stretch limited resources by eliminating problems.

Problems can hide in the shadows of your business.
Beware of old machinery and technology.
Beware of fast growing product lines.
Beware of big customers and suppliers.
Complicated procedures can harbor problems.
You must analyze your business closely.
You don't want to be surprised.

8—╾

Sometimes, the enemy is close by but remains calm.
Expect to find him in a natural stronghold.
Other times, he remains at a distance but provokes battle.
He wants you to attack him.

He sometimes shifts the position of his camp.
He is looking for an advantageous position.

The trees in the forest move.
Expect that the enemy is coming.
The tall grasses obstruct your view.
Be suspicious.

The birds take flight.
Expect that the enemy is hiding.
Animals startle.
Expect an ambush.

Notice the dust.
It sometimes rises high in a straight line.
Vehicles are coming.
The dust appears low in a wide band.
Foot soldiers are coming.
The dust seems scattered in different areas.
The enemy is collecting firewood.
Any dust is light and settling down.
The enemy is setting up camp.

78

Some problems happen frequently but are expected.
You must see that those problems are well entrenched.
Other problems are uncommon but get attention.
Don't let them distract your from more important issues.

Sometimes the cause of a problem seems to move around.
Solving it once and forever presents a real opportunity.

Well-established procedures become less consistent.
Expect that a change has occurred.
Productivity in some areas is hard to measure.
Distrust those areas.

Customers start to leave.
Look for hidden flaws that discourage them.
Some employees leave.
Expect problems they have hidden to appear.

Notice expenses.
Expenses can rise quickly in a specific area.
A sudden challenge is coming.
Expenses can rise generally across a broad area.
This means that your industry is getting more competitive.
Cost increases can be scattered throughout the business.
This means you are getting too comfortable.
Expense increases can be slight and fall down again.
This means that you have problems under control.

8━━★

Your enemy speaks humbly while building up forces.
He is planning to advance.

The enemy talks aggressively and pushes as if to advance.
He is planning to retreat.

Small vehicles exit his camp first and move to positions on
the army's flanks.
They are forming a battle line.

Your enemy tries to sue for peace but without offering a
treaty.
He is plotting.

Your enemy's men run to leave and yet form ranks.
You should expect action.

Half his army advances and the other half retreats.
He is luring you.

Your enemy plans to fight but his men just stand there.
They are starving.

Those who draw water drink it first.
They are thirsty.

Your enemy sees an advantage but does not advance.
His men are tired.

Birds gather.
Your enemy has abandoned his camp.

A problem can seem unimportant but keeps growing.
It will get more serious.

You worry about a potential problem and prepare for it.
That problem will be minimal.

Sudden changes in the business aggravate problems that
already exist.
You must address them.

Some problems seem to fade a little but never go away
entirely.
They will arise again.

Some problems seem easily resolved but reappear later.
You need to do more.

Do not solve problems only to create as many new ones.
This is a trap.

There are solutions that can not be implemented.
There are limits to resources.

You use technology to address your own issues first.
You are short-sighted.

There is an opportunity but you do not take advantage.
You are overworked.

New customers arrive.
This means that competitors are leaving them.

Your enemy's soldiers call in the night.
They are afraid.

Your enemy's army is raucous.
They do not take their commander seriously.

Your enemy's banners and flags shift.
Order is breaking down.

Your enemy's officers are irritable.
They are exhausted.

Your enemy's men kill their horses for meat.
They are out of provisions.

They don't put their pots away or return to their tents.
They expect to fight to the death.

Enemy troops appear sincere and agreeable.
But their men are slow to speak to each other.
They are no longer united.

Your enemy offers too many incentives to his men.
He is in trouble.

Your enemy gives out too many punishments.
His men are weary.

Your enemy first attacks and then is afraid of your larger
force.
His best troops have not arrived.

82

You have trouble sleeping at night
You are worried.

Your employees are undisciplined.
They don't take you seriously.

Competitors are reorganizing and giving out new titles.
Their organization is breaking down.

Your competitors' managers are short-tempered.
They are overworked.

Your competitors start selling assets.
Their operations are unprofitable.

Competitors don't clean up or go home at night.
They are trying to stay in business.

Your partners seem sincere and agreeable.
Nevertheless, they fail to communicate.
They do not see you as part of their team.

A business must offer incentives to get work done.
It is in trouble.

A business needs constantly to discipline its employees.
It is under pressure.

A competitor first attacks you and then quickly tries to
make friends.
He is waiting to learn more.

Your enemy comes in a conciliatory manner.
He needs to rest and recuperate.

Your enemy is angry and appears to welcome battle.
This goes on for a long time, but he doesn't attack.
He also doesn't leave the field.
You must watch him carefully.

If you are too weak to fight, you must find more men.
In this situation, you must not act aggressively.
You must unite your forces, expect the enemy, recruit men
and wait.

You must be cautious about making plans and adjust to the
enemy.
You must increase the size of your forces.

With new, undedicated soldiers, you can depend on them if
you discipline them.
They will tend to disobey your orders.
If they do not obey your orders, they will be useless.

You can depend on seasoned, dedicated soldiers.
But you must avoid disciplining them without reason.
Otherwise, you cannot use them.

You must control your soldiers with *esprit de corp*.
You must bring them together by winning victories.
You must get them to believe in you.

A competitor suggests a compromise solution.
He is simply buying time.

A competitor seems to want to steal your business.
He seems interested but does not go after your customers.
Nevertheless, he stays in the market.
You must keep your eye on him.

When stretched to the limit, you must hire more people.
At that time, you must not try to expand your business.
You must organize the business, train the new people, and
be patient.

You must plan carefully and work continually to improve
the business.
You must increase the size of your organization.

You can depend on new, untrained employees if you tell
them exactly what to do.
Otherwise, they will get confused.
If they are confused, they cannot be productive.

It is different with experienced, proven employees.
You must let them see for themselves what needs doing.
If they cannot, they are not good employees.

You must lead your employees by inspiring them.
You unite them by making them successful.
They must believe in you.

Make it easy for them to obey your orders by training your
people.
Your people will then obey you.
If you do not make it easy to obey, you won't train your
people.
Then they will not obey.

Make your commands easy to follow.
You must understand the way a crowd thinks.

Make it easy for emplyees to follow directions by training them well.
They will then do what is necessary.
If procedures are difficult to understand, you will not be able to train employees.
They will make too many mistakes.

Make your procedures easy to understand.
You must understand how groups of people work.

FIELD POSITION

Some field positions are unobstructed.
Some field positions are entangling.
Some field positions are supporting.
Some field positions are constricted.
Some field positions give you a barricade.
Some field positions are spread out.

You can attack from some positions easily.
Others can attack you easily as well.
We call these unobstructed positions.
These positions are open.
On them, be the first to occupy a high, sunny area.
Put yourself where you can defend your supply routes.
Then you will have an advantage.

CUSTOMER RELATIONSHIPS

Some customers are open-minded.
Some customers are selective.
Some customers are winnable.
Some customers are exclusive.
Some customers are closed-minded.
Some customers are unprofitable.

Some customers buy from you easily.
They will buy from the competition just as easily.
These are open-minded customers.
These customers are open to new ideas.
With these customers, be the first to understand their needs.
Work with them closely and position your business clearly.
With them, showing leadership is essential.

You can attack from some positions easily.
Disaster arises when you try to return to them.
These are entangling positions.
These field positions are one-sided.
Wait until your enemy is unprepared.
You can then attack from these positions and win.
Avoid a well prepared enemy.
You will try to attack and lose.
Since you can't return, you will meet disaster.
These field positions offer no advantage.

I cannot leave some positions without losing an advantage.
If the enemy leaves this ground, he also loses an advantage.
We call these supporting field positions.
These positions strengthen you.
The enemy may try to entice me away.
Still, I will hold my position.
You must entice the enemy to leave.
You then strike him as he is leaving.
These field positions offer an advantage.

Some field positions are constricted.
I try to get to these positions before the enemy does.
You must fill these areas and await the enemy.
Sometimes, the enemy will reach them first.
If he fills them, do not follow him.
But if he fails to fill them, you can go after him.

Some customers give you one shot at getting their business.
You cannot go back to them after striking out.
These are selective customers.
They give you one chance.
Wait and identify a problem that requires your help.
You can then go after them and win their business
Avoid selling to them if you do not have an edge.
Your attempts could fail.
Since you cannot come back, you waste your only chance.
You cannot control these customers.

Some customers go to whomever is the most persistent.
Neither you nor your competition can give up on them
without losing.
These are winnable customers.
Know when a customer is winnable.
You must stay with them.
If competition seems to give up, stay with the customer.
You must convince the competitors to lose patience.
You want this type of customer.

Some customers are exclusive.
You must interest these customers first.
You must win them and then not worry about competitors.
Your competitors may interest these customers first.
If competitors win over them over, do not waste your time.
But if competitors fail to win them, you can go after them.

Some field positions give you a barricade.
I get to these positions before the enemy does.
You occupy their southern, sunny heights and wait for the
enemy.
Sometimes the enemy occupies these areas first.
If so, entice him away.
Never go after him.

Some field positions are too spread out.
Your force may seem equal to the enemy.
Still you will lose if you provoke a battle.
If you fight, you will not have any advantage.

These are the six types of field positions.
Each battleground has its own rules.
As a commander, you must know where to go.
You must examine each position closely.

Some armies can be outmaneuvered.
Some armies are too lax.
Some armies fall down.
Some armies fall apart.
Some armies are disorganized.
Some armies must retreat.

Know all six of these weaknesses.
They lead to losses on both good and bad ground.
They all arise from the army's commander.

Some customers are closed-minded.
You must appeal to their prejudices before competitors do.
You must win them over exclusive and then suggest they
compare your products.
Sometimes your competitors seem to have won them first.
If so, see if you can entice them.
Never chase after them.

Some customers are unprofitable.
You can win their business from competitors.
But you are wasting your time with them.
Even if they buy, you will not make money on them.

These are the six types of customers.
Each customer type has its own rules.
You must know who your customers are.
You must never stop asking questions.

There are businesses that are beaten.
There are businesses that are too slow.
There are businesses that stumble.
There are businesses that fall apart.
There are businesses that are disorganized.
There are businesses that go bankrupt.

You must avoid these six pitfalls.
These weakness occur in both good and bad businesses.
They come from the business owner.

One general can command a force equal to the enemy.
Still his enemy outflanks him.
This means that his army can be outmaneuvered.

Another can have strong soldiers, but weak officers.
This means that his army will be too lax.

Another has strong officers but weak soldiers.
This means that his army will fall down.

Another has sub-commanders that are angry and defiant.
They attack the enemy and fight their own battles.
As a commander, he cannot know the battlefield.
This means that his army will fall apart.

Another general is weak and easygoing.
He fails to make his orders clear.
His officers and men lack direction,
This shows in his military formations.
This means that his army will be disorganized.

Another general fails to predict the enemy.
He pits his small forces against larger ones.
He puts his weak forces against stronger ones.
He fails to pick his fights correctly.
This means that his army must retreat.

You must know all about these six weaknesses.
You must understand the philosophies that lead to defeat.
When a general arrives, you can know what he will do.
You must study each one carefully.

94

Your business may be equal to a competing business.
Still, you let competitors take your customers.
This means that your business can be beaten.

Your ideas are good, but you do not work hard.
Your business will be too slow.

You work hard but your ideas are weak.
Your business will stumble.

You have partners who are emotional and independent.
They do what they please in the business.
As the manager, you do not know what is going on.
Your business will fall apart.

You can be lazy and sloppy.
You fail to make your priorities clear.
Your actions lack focus.
Your time is not well spent.
Your business is disorganized.

As an owner, you can fail to predict sales.
You spend money on ideas that do not create sales.
You sell unprofitable products instead of profitable ones.
You fail to pick the right customers.
Your business must eventually go bankrupt.

You must understand all six business weaknesses.
You must understand the mindset that leads to failure.
When customers come, you must know what to do.
You must study each one carefully.

You must control your field position.
It will always strengthen your army.

You must predict the enemy to overpower him and win.
You must analyze the obstacles, dangers, and distances.
This is the best way to command.

Understand your field position before you go to battle.
Then you will win.
You can fail to understand your field position and still fight.
Then you will lose.

You must provoke battle when you will certainly win.
It doesn't matter what you are ordered.
The government may order you not to fight.
Despite that, you must always fight when you will win.

Sometimes provoking a battle will lead to a loss.
The government may order you to fight.
Despite that, you must avoid battle when you will lose.

You must advance without desiring praise.
You must retreat without fearing shame.
The only correct move is to preserve your troops.
This is how you serve your country.
This is how you reward your nation.

You must guide the customer.
This always strengthens your business.

You must foresee how to undermine the competition.
You must analyze customers' problems and needs.
This is the best way to start a business.

You must understand these issues when you run a business.
If you do, you will always succeed.
You may not understand these issues and try to do business.
Your business will always fail.

You must ask for an order when you are will get the sale.
Do not try to time the sale to meet your business's needs.
There may be many reasons why the timing isn't ideal.
Still, you must close a sale when the opportunity is there.

When you will lose a sale, you must delay the decision.
You may need the business badly and immediately.
Still, you must delay a decision that you will lose.

You must never sell simply because you need cash.
You must ask for orders without worrying about rejection.
Do what you need to preserve your business.
You must help the customers to help your business.
This is how you make your business successful.

Think of your soldiers as little children.
You can make them follow you into a deep river.
Treat them as your beloved children.
You can lead them all to their deaths.

Some leaders are generous, but cannot use their men.
They love their men, but cannot command them.
Their men are unruly and disorganized.
These leaders create spoiled children.
Their soldiers are useless.

You may know what your soldiers will do in an attack.
You may not know if the enemy is vulnerable to attack.
You will then win only half the time.
You may know that the enemy is vulnerable to attack.
You may not know if your men are capable of attacking them.
You will still win only half the time.
You may know that the enemy is vulnerable to attack.
You may know that your men are ready to attack.
You may not know how to position yourself in the field for battle.
You will still win only half the time.

You must know how to make war.
You can then act without confusion.
You can attempt anything.

Treat your customers as your children.
They will stay with you.
Treat them with care and attention.
You can keep them forever.

Some business owners are generous with their customers.
They love customers but cannot profit from them.
Their business is confused and disorganized.
These owners create impossible expectations.
Their businesses are hopeless.

8—ᛝ

You can know that you offer good products and services.
But you must also understand their value to the customer.
If you do not, you have only done half your job.
You can know how to satisfy customer needs.
But you must still convince customers that your products
are worth the price.
If you do not, you have only done half your job.
You can know customers' needs.
You can know how your products serve their needs.
But you must also know how to make money from selling
your products.
If you do not, you have done only half your job.

You must truly understand how your business works.
You can then act with certainty.
The sky is the limit.

We say:
Know the enemy and know yourself.
Your victory will be painless.
Know the weather and the field.
Your victory will be complete.

Pay attention:
Know your customers and your business.
Then success is effortless.
Understand customers' thinking and their needs.
Then your success is assured.

TYPES OF TERRAIN

Use the art of war.
Know when the terrain will scatter you.
Know when the terrain will be easy.
Know when the terrain will be disputed.
Know when the terrain is open.
Know when the terrain is intersecting.
Know when the terrain is dangerous.
Know when the terrain is bad.
Know when the terrain is confined.
Know when the terrain is deadly.

Warring parties must sometimes fight inside their own
territory.
This is scattering terrain.

When you enter hostile territory, your penetration is shallow.
This is easy terrain.

Some terrain gives me an advantageous position.
However, it gives others an advantageous position as well.
This will be disputed terrain.

STAGES OF BUSINESS

Use your business sense:
Know when business is tenuous.
Know when business is easy.
Know when business is contentious.
Know when business is open.
Know when business is shared.
Know when business is serious.
Know when business is difficult.
Know when business is limited.
Know when business is do-or-die.

You must sometimes defend against a new competitor in
your market.
This is the tenuous stage.

When you move into a new market, your business is new.
This is the easy stage.

Some customers give you great sales.
Nevertheless, competitors can win great sales as well.
This is the contentious stage.

I can use some terrain to advance easily.
Others, however, can use it to move against me.
This is open terrain.

Everyone shares access to a given area.
The first one there can gather a larger group than anyone
else.
This is intersecting terrain.

You can penetrate deeply into hostile territory.
Then many hostile cities are behind you.
This is dangerous terrain.

There are mountain forests.
There are rugged hills.
There are marshes.
Everyone confronts these obstacles on a campaign.
They make bad terrain.

In some areas, the passage is narrow.
You are closed in as you enter and exit them.
In this type of area, a few people can attack our much larger
force.
This is confined terrain.

You can sometimes survive only if you fight quickly.
You will die if you delay.
This is deadly terrain.

You make easy progress building your business.
Competitors, however, can still come in at any time.
This is the open stage.

Several non-competing companies sell to your customers.
If you can develop good partnerships, you will dominate
the market.
This is the shared stage.

You invest heavily to build you business.
Competitors have many devoted customers in the market.
This is the serious stage.

Business slows down.
Distributors are lost.
Key customers leave you.
Every company encounters these situations.
This is the difficult stage.

In some businesses, there is a key transition point.
You have a few key employees, customers, or distributors.
Your entire business can be lost if competitors know how
dependent you are.
This is the limited stage.

You can win only if you commit all your resources.
You will lose your business if you delay.
This is the do-or-die stage.

To be successful, you control scattering terrain by not
fighting.
Control easy terrain by not stopping.
Control disputed terrain by not attacking.
Control open terrain by staying with the enemy's forces.
Control intersecting terrain by uniting with your allies.
Control dangerous terrain by plundering.
Control bad terrain by keeping on the move.
Control confined terrain by using surprise.
Control deadly terrain by fighting.

Go to any area that helps you in waging war.
You use it to cut off the enemy's contact between his front
and back lines.
Prevent his small parties from relying on his larger force.
Stop his strong divisions from rescuing his weak ones.
Prevent his officers from getting his men together.
Chase his soldiers apart to stop them from amassing.
Harass them to prevent their ranks from forming.

When joining battle gives you an advantage, you must do it.
When it isn't to your benefit, you must avoid it.

A daring soldier may ask:
"A large, organized enemy army and its general are coming.
What do I do to prepare for them?"

To be successful, avoid the tenuous stage by not leaving openings for competitors.
During the easy stage, do not stop building your business.
During the contentious stage, avoid the competition.
In the open stage, keep up with competitors.
In the shared stage, make good alliances.
In the serious stage, concentrate on generating income.
In the difficult stage, keep your business adapting.
In the limited stage, be inventive.
In the do-or-die stage, fight to win.

Find the customers to whom you are the most valuable.
Use targeted marketing to prevent larger competitors from bringing their power against you.
Choose niches where competitors' size works against them.
Choose areas where competitors have little skill.
Mislead their leaders about the value of your target market.
Stop any business that they might do with your customers.
Prevent competitors from copying your methods.

When you have an obvious advantage, force comparisons.
When you do not have an advantage, avoid comparisons.

You wonder:
"A big, organized competitor is coming into my market. What should I do?"

Tell him:
"First seize an area that the enemy must have.
Then they will pay attention to you.
Mastering speed is the essence of war.
Take advantage of a large enemy's inability to keep up.
Use a philosophy of avoiding difficult situations.
Attack the area where he doesn't expect you."

You must use the philosophy of an invader.
Invade deeply and then concentrate your forces.
This controls your men without oppressing them.

Get your supplies from the riches of the territory.
It is sufficient to supply your whole army.

Take care of your men and do not overtax them.
Your *esprit de corps* increases your momentum.
Keep your army moving and plan for surprises.
Make it difficult for the enemy to count your forces.
Position your men where there is no place to run.
They will then face death without fleeing.
They will find a way to survive.
Your officers and men will fight to their utmost.

Military officers that are completely committed lose their fear.
When they have nowhere to run, they must stand firm.
Deep in enemy territory, they are captives.
Since they cannot escape, they will fight.

There is an answer.
First, attack the competitor in an area that they value more.
Then the competitor must pay attention to that area.
You can quickly change your business focus.
Take advantage of a large competitor's inability to refocus.
Avoid investing where you will have real opposition.
Keep your business where the competition is unprepared.

Your business must live off selling to its customers.
Commit totally to your customers and win their business.
This focuses your business without limiting it.

You must generate profits quickly from your market.
Profits alone can pay for all your business growth.

Take care of employees and do not overburden them.
Share your company's success with your people.
Keep your people busy and expecting surprises.
Make it difficult for competitors to steal your people.
Create a business that holds experienced employees.
They must stay with you even when problems arise.
Dependent people find solutions to problems.
If people are dependent, they will work hard for you.

When people are dependent on you, they lose their fear.
When they have no alternatives, they will stay with you.
Committed to your customers, employees will stay.
Since they have nowhere else to go, they will work hard.

Commit your men completely.
Without being posted, they will be on guard.
Without being asked, they will get what is needed.
Without being forced, they will be dedicated.
Without being given orders, they can be trusted.

Stop them from guessing by removing all their doubts.
Stop them from dying by giving them no place to run.

Your officers may not be rich.
Nevertheless, they still desire plunder.
They may die young.
Nevertheless, they still want to live forever.

You must order the time of attack.
Officers and men may sit and weep until their lapels are wet.
When they stand up, tears may stream down their cheeks.
Put them in a position where they cannot run.
They will show the greatest courage under fire.

Make good use of war.
This demands instant reflexes.
You must develop these instant reflexes.
Act like an ordinary mountain snake.
Someone can strike at your head.
You can then attack with your tail
Someone can strike at your tail.
You can then attack with your head.
Someone can strike at your middle.
You can then attack with both your head and tail.

110

Commit your employees completely.
Without being told, everyone must know what to do.
Without being asked, everyone must see what is needed.
Without being forced, everyone must be dedicated.
Without being instructed, everyone must be trusted.

Stop any second-guessing by making commitments clear.
Avoid failure by leaving your people no excuses.

You and your people may not be rich.
This is not because you do not want to win wealth.
You may all fail.
It should not be because you did not commit to success.

You must know the time when work must get done.
Everyone will complain that they cannot meet deadlines.
When they must finish, they will tell you that they cannot.
Put them in a position where they have no choice.
They will find a way to get the work done.

Make good use of the stage of business you are in.
Business demands quick reflexes.
You must prepare to overcome problems instantly.
You should be able to act on instinct.
Competitors will challenge your business's concept.
Attack the competition for being outdated.
Competitors will challenge you for being too late.
Attack the competitors for being too hasty.
Competitors can challenge you on any issue.
Immediately respond with attacks of your own.

111

A daring soldier asks:
"Can any army imitate these instant reflexes?"
We answer:
"It can."

To command and get the most of proud people, you must
study adversity.
People work together when they are in the same boat during a
storm.
In this situation, one rescues the other just as the right hand
helps the left.

Use adversity correctly.
Tether your horses and bury your wagon's wheels.
Still, you can't depend on this alone.
An organized force is braver than lone individuals.
This is the art of organization.
Put the tough and weak together.
You must also use the terrain.

Make good use of war.
Unite your men as one.
Never let them give up.

The commander must be a military professional.
This requires confidence and detachment.
You must maintain dignity and order.
You must control what your men see and hear.
They must follow you without knowing your plans.

You may question these reflexes.
Should your business respond instantly to attack?
There is only one answer.
You must!

To lead and control employees, you must understand how
to use adversity.
You must bind your people together by giving them
challenges to conquer.
You will work together when everyone realizes that you all
share in the difficulty.

Use challenges correctly.
Tie your future together with your employees.
Even this is not enough.
A team is more courageous than any individual.
This is the art of teamwork.
You must tie your best and worst employees together.
You must use your business stage.

Make good use of business activity.
Unite your people as one.
Never let them quit.

$\vdash$

A business owner must be a professional.
This requires confidence and detachment.
You must maintain your leadership and focus.
You must control what your employees see and hear.
They must believe in you without knowing your plans.

You can reinvent your men's roles.
You can change your plans.
You can use your men without their understanding.

You must shift your campgrounds.
You must take detours from the ordinary routes.
You must use your men without giving them your strategy.

A commander provides what his army needs now.
You must be willing to climb high and then kick away your
ladder.
You must be able to lead your men deeply into your enemy's
territory and then find a way to create the opportunity that
you need.

You must drive men like a flock of sheep.

You must drive them to march.
You must drive them to attack.
You must never let them know where you are headed.
You must unite them into a great army.
You must then drive them against all opposition.
This is the job of a true commander.

You must adapt to the different terrain.
You must adapt to find an advantage.
You must manage your people's affections.
You must study all these skills.

You can reinvent people's jobs.
You can change the plans.
You must lead people without having to explain everything.

You must be able to change your location.
You must be able change your business procedures.
Your people must accept change explaining everything.

You must provide exactly what people need at the moment.
You must be willing to go out on a limb and take a risk in your business.
You must get your employees deeply involved with your customers to discover the problems creating the opportunities for success.

You must guide your people like a flock of sheep.

You must inspire them to move.
You must entice them to work.
You must not let them take their jobs for granted.
You must unite them into a powerful, productive machine.
You must set them against your competitors.
This is the job of a true business leader.

You must adapt to every business stage.
You must adjust your methods to win customers.
You must win on your employees' affections.
You must learn all these skills.

Always use the philosophy of invasion.
Deep invasions concentrate your forces.
Shallow invasions scatter your forces.
When you leave your country and cross the border, you must take control.
This is always critical ground.
You can sometimes move in any direction.
This is always intersecting ground.
You can penetrate deeply into a territory.
This is always dangerous ground.
You penetrate only a little way.
This is always easy ground.
Your retreat is closed and the path ahead tight.
This is always confined ground.
There is sometimes no place to run.
This is always deadly ground.

To use scattering terrain correctly, we must inspire our men's devotion.
On easy terrain, we must keep in close communication.
On disputed terrain, we should try to hamper the enemy's progress.
On open terrain, we must carefully defend our chosen position.
On intersecting terrain, we must solidify our alliances.
On dangerous terrain, we must ensure our food supplies.
On bad terrain, we must keep advancing along the road.
On confined terrain, we must barricade a stronghold on the high ground.
On deadly terrain, we must show what we can do by killing the enemy.

Your business must generate profit from its customers.
Commitment to your customers focuses your efforts.
Lack of commitment dissipates your resources.
At the beginning of starting your business, you must take the lead.
This is a critical time.
You and other businesses can have goals in common.
This is the shared stage.
You can invest everything in the business in a new market.
This is always the serious stage.
All businesses look promising when you first start in them.
This is always the easy stage of a business.
A business can narrow until you must rely on a few people.
This is the limited stage of a business.
A business can depend on what happens now.
This is the do-or-die stage.

To succeed in the tenuous stage, you must have your employees' devotion.
In the easy stage, you must communicate with customers.
In the contentious stage, you must create obstacles for your competitors.
In the open stage, you must defend your business's value to its customers.
In the shared stage, you must join your partners.
In the serious stage, you must generate profits.
In the difficult stage, you must keep the business adapting.
In the limited stage, you must keep your relationship with key people.
In the do-or-die stage, you must prove yourself by overcoming the challenge at hand.

117

Make your men feel like an army.
Surround them and they will defend themselves.
If they cannot avoid it, they will fight.
If they are under pressure, they will obey.

Do the right thing when you don't know your different
enemies' plans.
Don't attempt to meet them.

You don't know the local mountains, forests, hills and
marshes?
Then you cannot march the army.
You don't have local guides?
You won't get any of the benefits of the terrain.

There are many factors in war.
You may lack knowledge of any one of them.
If so, it is wrong to take a nation into war.

You must be able to dominate a nation at war.
Divide a big nation before they are able to gather a large
force.
Increase your enemy's fear.
Prevent his forces from getting together and organizing.

Do the right thing and don't try to compete for outside
alliances.
You won't have to fight for authority.
Trust only yourself and your own resources.
This increases the enemy's uncertainty.
You can force one of his allies to pull out.
His whole nation can fall.

Make your business team powerful.
If they are focused on the customer, they will succeed.
When they have no choice, they will work.
When they are pressured, they will follow your lead.

Do the right thing when you do not understand the
customers' thinking.
Do not try to win their business.

You do not understand your customers' buying habits,
tastes, and needs?
Then you cannot start a business.
You do not know your market?
You will not know your customers' thinking or needs.

There is so much to know to start a business.
You do not want to miss anything.
Otherwise, you cannot control the growth of the business.

You must keep large competitors out of your market.
Steal away their ideas and momentum before they can
establish a foothold.
Increase their disappointment in the market.
Prevent them from developing partners and an organization.

Do the right thing and do not always depend on partners to
help with every market.
Then you will not have to fight for leadership.
Trust yourself and your own resources.
This decreases any competitor's source of information.
You may convince your competitor's allies to abandon him.
His whole business can then collapse.

Distribute plunder without worrying about agreements.
Halt without the government's command.
Attack with the whole strength of your army.
Use your army as if it was a single man.

Attack with skill.
Do not discuss it.
Attack when you have an advantage.
Do not talk about the dangers.
When you can launch your army into deadly ground, even if
it stumbles, it can still survive.
You can be weakened in a deadly battle and yet be stronger
afterward.

Even a large force can fall into misfortune.
If you fall behind, however, you can still turn defeat into
victory.
You must use the skills of war.
To survive, you must adapt to your enemy's purpose.
You must stay with him no matter where he goes.
It may take a thousand miles to kill the general.
If you correctly understand him, you can find the skill to do
it.

Manage your government correctly at the start of a war.
Close your borders and tear up passports.
Block the passage of envoys.
Encourage politicians at headquarters to stay out of it.
You must use any means to put an end to politics.
Your enemy's people will leave you an opening.
You must instantly invade through it.

Working alone, you do not have politics.
You can change your offerings without discussion.
You can focus all your resources on the target customer.
You can work with a single goal.

Do business with skill.
Do not expose your plans.
Be aggressive when you find an edge.
Do not advertise the risks.
You can go through difficult stages and lose customers, but
you can still survive.
You may lose ground in a competitive market, but you can
also learn from your mistakes.

You can win many times and still get into bad situations.
If you make mistakes, you can still turn initial failure into
ultimate success.
You must use your business skills.
You must adapt completely to business conditions.
You must keep up with your customers no matter what.
You can turn customers around and win their business.
If you understand a customer's options, you can find a way
to win him.

Do the right things at the start of a business.
Protect existing markets and keep competitors out.
Prevent your plans from getting out.
Get the complete commitment of your employees.
Eliminate anything that disturbs your business's focus.
Identify competitors' weaknesses.
Quickly take advantage of these weaknesses.

121

Immediately seize a place that they love.
Do it quickly.
Trample any border to pursue the enemy.
Use your judgment about when to fight.

Doing the right thing at the start of war is like approaching a woman.
Your enemy's men must open the door.
After that, you should act like a streaking rabbit.
The enemy will be unable to catch you.

Quickly win a customer base for your business.
Waste no time.
Break down any barriers to winning customers.
Use your best judgment about where to compete.

Success at the beginning comes from wooing your
customers like you woo a woman.
Your competitors will eventually neglect her.
When they do, you should act quickly.
Never let your competitors catch up with you.

ATTACKING WITH FIRE

There are five ways of attacking with fire.
The first is burning troops.
The second is burning supplies.
The third is burning supply transport.
The fourth is burning storehouses.
The fifth is burning camps.

To make fire, you must have the resources.
To build a fire, you must prepare the raw materials.

To attack with fire, you must be in the right season.
To start a fire, you must have the time.

Choose the right season.
The weather must be very dry.

Choose the right time.
Pick a season when the grass is as high as the side of a cart.

You can tell the proper days by the stars in the night sky.
You want days when the wind rises in the morning.

IMPROVING BUSINESS PRODUCTIVITY

There are five ways to improve business productivity.
First, you can speed operations.
Second, you can improve supply.
Third, you can speed delivery.
Fourth, you can eliminate storage.
Fifth, you can emphasize communication.

To improve business productivity, you need resources.
To make a change, you must prepare new methods.

To improve quickness, you must synchronize processes.
To speed your operations, you invest time to do it.

Choose the right season.
The trends must be predictable.

Choose the right time.
Make changes when your business is prepared.

You can know when to change by studying the signs.
Wait for a time when the business environment supports it.

Everyone attacks with fire.
You must create five different situations with fire and be able
to adjust to them.

You start a fire inside the enemy's camp.
Then attack the enemy's periphery.

You launch a fire attack, but the enemy remains calm.
Wait and do not attack.

The fire reaches its height.
Follow its path if you can.
If you can't follow it, stay where you are.

Spreading fires on the outside of camp can kill.
You can't always get fire inside the enemy's camp.
Take your time in spreading it.

Set the fire when the wind is at your back.
Don't attack into the wind.
Daytime winds last a long time.
Night winds fade quickly.

Every army must know how to deal with the five attacks by
fire.
Use many men to guard against them.

Everyone tries to improve business productivity.
You must master five different approaches to improve your efficiency.

You can directly eliminate certain tasks.
To do this, change the processes around them.

If you eliminate a task, you may have no problem at first.
Wait before making more changes.

The time a task takes naturally expands.
Keep a history of the time tasks if you can.
If you don't understand a task, avoid making changes.

Making small changes in a procedure can work.
Do not eliminate the task; speed it.
Be patient in automating jobs.

Make sure that other processes work with your change.
Do not save time in one place to only lose it in another.
Dramatic improvements last a long time.
Subtle ones fade quickly.

You must master these five rules to improve business productivity.
Use your employess to invent new ideas.

When you use fire to assist your attacks, you are being
clever.
Water can add force to an attack.
You can also use water to disrupt an enemy.
It doesn't, however, take his resources.

You win in battle by getting the opportunity to attack.
It is dangerous if you fail to study how to accomplish this
achievement.
As commander, you cannot waste your opportunities.

We say:
A wise leader plans success.
A good general studies it.
If there is little to be gained, don't act.
If there is little to win, do not use your men.
If there is no danger, don't fight.

As leader, you cannot let your anger interfere with the success
of your forces.
As commander, you cannot fight simply because you are
enraged.
Join the battle only when it is in your advantage to act.
If there is no advantage in joining a battle, stay put.

Anger can change back into happiness.
Rage can change back into joy.
A nation once destroyed cannot be brought back to life.
Dead men do not return to the living.

When you improve your business's productivity, you always create value.
Technology can provide the impetus for change.
Using technology can eliminate work.
Because of its costs, it does not always create value.

8—⊼

You succeed in any organization by improving.
It is a mistake if you don't look for opportunities to innovate.
In starting a business, you cannot waste any opportunity.

This much is true:
If you are smart, you plan to succeed.
If you are clever, you examine your business.
If a change is not worth the effort, do not attempt it.
If it cannot make a difference, do not waste your efforts.
If there is no real problem, you cannot address it.

You must never let your emotions affect the success of your business.
You must never make changes simply because you are upset.
Do only what is needed to improve productivity.
If there is no profit in innovation, keep away from it.

Something that upsets you may one day make you happy.
Anger can change to joy.
If you destroy the business, there is no second chance.
Employees that quit do not come back.

This fact must make a wise leader cautious.
A good general is on guard.

Your philosophy must be to keep the nation peaceful and the army intact.

Knowing this, you must be careful.
A good business owner is careful.

Your plan must be to keep the organization together and
your employees happy.

Using Spies

Altogether, building an army requires thousands of men.
They invade and march thousands of miles.
Whole families are destroyed.
Other families must be heavily taxed.
Every day, thousands of dollars must be spent.

Internal and external events force people to move.
They are unable to work while on the road.
They are unable to find and hold a useful job.
This affects seventy percent of thousands of families.

You can watch and guard for years.
Then a single battle can determine victory in a day.
Despite this, bureaucrats hold onto their salary money too
dearly.
They remain ignorant of the enemy's condition.
The result is cruel.

They are not leaders of men.
They are not servants of the state.
They are not masters of victory.

Using Information

Starting a business involves thousands of people.
People labor and work thousands of hours.
They invest a large part of their lives in their business.
Many invest their life's savings.
Every day, businesses consume resources.

Internal and external events force businesses to shut down.
Productivity is lost as their employees search for new work.
Many are unable to find jobs that are as productive.
Eighty percents of new business fail within two years.

You can run a business for years.
Then a single opportunity can determine its success.
Despite this, many business owners invest money in salaries.
They don't invest in information.
The result is devastating.

Without information, you cannot start a business.
You cannot create value for customers.
You cannot be successful.

You need a creative leader and a worthy commander.
You must move your troops to the right places to beat others.
You must accomplish your attack and escape unharmed.
This requires foreknowledge.
You can obtain foreknowledge.
You can't get it from demons or spirits.
You can't see it from professional experience.
You can't check it with analysis.
You can only get it from other people.
You must always know the enemy's situation.

You must use five types of spies.
You need local spies.
You need inside spies.
You need double agents.
You need doomed spies.
You need surviving spies.

You need all five types of spies.
No one must discover your methods.
You will be then able to put together a true picture.
This is the commander's most valuable resource.

You need local spies.
Get them by hiring people from the countryside.

You need inside spies.
Win them by subverting government officials.

You need double agents.
Discover enemy agents and convert them.

You must create a valuable and productive business.
You must put your resources in the right places.
You must survive in a competitive environment.
This requires information.
You can get this information.
You will not get it from philosophy.
You will not get it from past experience.
You cannot reason it out.
You can only get it by collecting it from other people.
You must always know your business situation.

You need five types of information.
You need market information.
You need customer information.
You need competitor information.
You need marketing information.
You need sales information.

You must use all five types of information.
If you do, no one can challenge your business.
You understand your business and its position.
Information is your most valuable resource.

You need information on the marketplace.
Win it by asking your customers questions.

You need information on specific customers.
Find out what others know about their purchases.

You need information on competitive methods.
Hire people from other organizations and use them.

You need doomed spies.
Deceive professionals into being captured.
We let them know our orders.
They then take those orders to our enemy.

You need surviving spies.
Someone must return with a report.

Your job is to build a complete army.
No relations are as intimate as they are with spies.
No rewards are too generous for spies.
No work is as secret as that of spies.

If you aren't clever and wise, you can't use spies.
If you aren't fair and just, you can't use spies.
If you can't see the tiny subtleties, you won't get the truth
from spies.

Pay attention to small, trifling details!
Spies are helpful in every area.

Spies are the first to hear information, so they must not
spread it.
Spies who give your location or talk to others must be killed
along with those to whom they have talked.

You need marketing information.
You must make the marketplace aware of your business.
Let them know your value.
Promote and advertise your business in the marketplace.

You need sales information.
Someone must analyze which sales are making money.

Your job is to build a complete organization.
No resources are as critical as information sources.
No reward is too generous for critical information.
No information is as hard to win as timely information.

You must be smart enough to correlate data.
You must be open and unbiased to evaluate it.
If you aren't sensitive to subtleties, you will not find the truth in information.

You must pay close attention to small details.
Information is helpful in every area.

Your people must gather information, but they must not spread it.
People that divulge your plans or successes to opponents can destroy you.

You may want to attack an army's position.
You may want to attack a certain fortification.
You may want to kill people in a certain place.
You must first know the guarding general.
You must know his left and right flanks.
You must know his hierarchy.
You must know the way in.
You must know where different people are stationed.
We must demand this information from our spies.

I want to know the enemy spies in order to convert new spies into my men.
You find a source of information and bribe them.
You must bring them in with you.
You must obtain them as double agents and use them as your emissaries.

Do this correctly and carefully.
You can contact both local and inside spies and obtain their support.
Do this correctly and carefully.
You create doomed spies by deceiving professionals.
You can use them to give false information.
Do this correctly and carefully.
You must have surviving spies capable of bringing you information at the right time.

You may want to copy your competitor's best practices.
You may want to offer a new product.
You may want to stop offering a service.
You must first know what customers think.
You must know how other businesses are organized.
You must know your priorities.
You must know where opportunities are.
You must know how people work together.
You must get this information from real people.

You want to know who understands competitors' practices
and hire them.
You must be willing to pay for information.
You must attract knowledgeable people to you.
You must win people with outside experience and use them
to attract others.

You must do this carefully.
You can hire from your competitors and win competitive
knowledge.
You must also do this selectively.
You create marketing information by using media.
You get the media interested by enticing them.
You must do this carefully as well.
You need detailed information on what you are selling at all
times.

These are the five different types of intelligence work.
You must be certain to master them all.
You must be certain to create double agents.
You cannot afford to be too cheap in creating these double
agents.

This technique created the success of ancient emperors.
This is how they held their dynasties.

You must always be careful of your success.
Learn from the past examples.

Be a smart commander and good general.
You do this by using your best and brightest people for
spying.
This is how you achieve the greatest success.
This is how you meet the necessities of war.
The whole army's position and ability to move depends on
these spies.

There are five different types of information.
You must be certain to use them all.
You must be certain to understand competitive practices.
You cannot invest too much time in understanding the best practices.

This is how owners create successful business.
This is how they have beaten competitors.

You must always be careful of your success.
Learn from the history of commerce.

You must be an informed and capable business owner.
You must use your best and brightest people to gather information.
This is how you achieve the greatest success.
This is how you satisfy the needs of your business.
Your whole business's position and ability depends on good information.

The *Art of War Plus* Series

Competor's Guides for Business and Career

Sun Tzu's **The Art of War *Plus* The Art of Career Building**

$14.95 160 Pages. Paperback, 5 1/2" X 8 1/2". By Gary Gagliardi.
The Art of War plus an adaptation that applies Sun Tzu's lessons to the life-long process of advancing your professional career. *The Art of War* is shown on the left-hand page; its adaptation as *The Art of Career Building* is on the right-hand page. ISBN: 1929194137.

Sun Tzu's **The Art of War *Plus* The Art of Starting a Business**

$14.95 160 Pages. Paperback, 5 1/2" X 8 1/2". By Gary Gagliardi.
The Art of War plus an adaptation that applies Sun Tzu's lessons to all the challenges of starting a new business in the modern marketplace. *The Art of War* is shown on the left-hand page; its adaptation as *The Art of Starting a Business* is on the right-hand page. ISBN: 1929194153.

Sun Tzu's **The Art of War *Plus* The Art of Sales**

$14.95 160 Pages. Paperback, 5 1/2" X 8 1/2". By Gary Gagliardi.
The Art of War plus an adaptation for sales people that applies Sun Tzu's lessons to common sales situations. *The Art of War* is shown on the left-hand page; its adaptation as *The Art of Sales* is on the right-hand page. ISBN: 1929194013.

Sun Tzu's **The Art of War *Plus* The Art of Management**

$14.95 160 Pages. Paperback, 5 1/2" X 8 1/2". By Gary Gagliardi.
The Art of War plus an adaptation for organization managers that applies Sun Tzu's lessons to managing people, resources, and quality in a modern organization. *The Art of War* is shown on the left-hand page; its adaptation as *The Art of Management* is on the right-hand page. ISBN: 1929194056.

Sun Tzu's **The Art of War *Plus* The Art of Marketing**

$14.95 160 Pages. Paperback, 5 1/2" X 8 1/2". By Gary Gagliardi.
The Art of War plus an adaptation that applies Sun Tzu's lessons to winning modern marketing warfare. *The Art of War* is shown on the left-hand page; its adaptation as *The Art of Marketing* is on the right-hand page. ISBN: 1929194021.

Competitor's Guides for Mastering Sun Tzu

Sun Tzu's **The Art of War** *Plus* **Sun Tzu's Own Words**

$9.95 160 Pages. Paperback, 5 1/2" X 8 1/2". Translated by Gary Gagliardi. The most accurate translation of the ancient classic. A character by character translation of the Chinese ideograms is on the left-hand page. The corresponding English sentences are on the facing right-hand page. ISBN 1929194005

Sun Tzu's **The Art of War** *Plus* **The Amazing Secrets of Sun Tzu**

$14.95 160 Pages.   Paperback, 5 1/2" X 8 1/2". By Gary Gagliardi The best explanation of the hidden elements in the text. The complete text of *The Art of War* on the left-hand page. On the facing right-hand page, the secrets hidden in the text are explained in words and pictures. ISBN 1929194072.

Sun Tzu's **The Art of War** *Plus* **The Warrior Class**

$29.95 320 Pages. Paperback, 5 1/2" X 8 1/2". By Gary Gagliardi An detailed discussion of each stanza of Sun Tzu's *The Art of War*. Each stanza is explained in depth for its use in modern competition. ISBN: 1929194099.

Competitor's Guides for Your Personal Life
(Available Summer, 2002)

Sun Tzu's **The Art of War** *Plus* **The Art of Wanning Love**

$14.95 160 Pages. Paperback, 5 1/2" X 8 1/2". By Gary Gagliardi *The Art of War* plus an adaptation for findng, winning, and holding onto a life-long love. *The Art of War* is shown on the left-hand page; its adaptation as *The Art of Winning Love* is on the right-hand page. ISBN: 1929194145.

Sun Tzu's **The Art of War** *Plus* **The Art of Parenting Teens**

$14.95 160 Pages.   Paperback, 5 1/2" X 8 1/2". By Gary Gagliardi *The Art of War* plus an adaptation for keeping your teen alive and well until you can get them safely out of the house. *The Art of War* is shown on the left-hand page; its adaptation as *The Art of Parenting Teenages* is on the right-hand page. ISBN: 1929194161.

More Competitor's Guides Planned!
Check www.clearbridge.com for the latest information!

Audio and Video

Amazing Secrets of Sun Tzu's The Art of War VIDEO
Plus Amazing Secrets Companion Book
$49.95. 1 1/2 Hours. VHS. 160-Page Book by Gary Gagliardi.
A video recording of a live presentation by Gary Gagliardi on the sophisticated system of competition hidden in Sun Tzu's *The Art of War*. The book, *The Art of War Plus The Amazing Secrets of Sun Tzu,* contains the complete *Art of War* text and a detailed explanation of the seminar topic, ISBN 1929194110. Video without book $39.95, ISBN 1929194080.

Amazing Secrets of Sun Tzu's The Art of War CD SET
Plus Amazing Secrets Companion Book
$39.95. 1 1/2 Hours. Set: Two CDs. 160-Page Book by Gary Gagliardi.
A recording of a live presentation by Gary Gagliardi on the sophisticated system of competition hidden in Sun Tzu The Art of War. The book, *The Art of War Plus The Amazing Secrets of Sun Tzu,* contains the complete *Art of War* text and detailed explanation of the seminar topic. ISBN 1929194129. CD Set without book $29.95, ISBN 1929194102.

Speaking and Training
Gary Gagliardi, the author of **The Art of War *Plus*** series, is available for a *limited* number of speaking engagements. Contact Becky Wilson at Clearbridge Publishing: 206-533-9357.

Volume Discounts
All Clearbridge titles are available at a discount when purchased in quantity. Titles can be combined to qualify for discounts.

Discount Schedule

Total # of Items	Percentage Discount
5-9	15%
10-49	30%
50-99	40%
100-249	45%
250-499	46%
500-990	48%

Fax orders to Clearbridge. FAX: 206-546-9756.

Clearbridge Order Form
Fax 206-546-9756

Company Name:_____

Contact Person:_____

Shipping Address:_____

City State Zip:_____
Phone Number: _____ Fax Number: _____

Quantity	ISBN	Title	Retail	Total Retail
_____	1929194005	AOW & Sun Tzu's Own Words	$9.95	_____
_____	1929194013	AOW & The Art of Sales	$14.95	_____
_____	1929194021	AOW & The Art of Marketing	$14.95	_____
_____	1929194056	AOW & The Art of Management	$14.95	_____
_____	1929194072	AOW & Amazing Secrets of Sun Tzu	$14.95	_____
_____	1929194099	AOW & The Warrior Class	$29.95	_____
_____	1929194137	AOW & The Art of Career Building	$14.95	_____
_____	1929194145	AOW & The Art of Winning Love	$14.95	_____
_____	1929194153	AOW & The Art of Starting a Business	$14.95	_____
_____	1929194161	AOW & The Art of Parenting Teens	$14.95	_____
_____	1929194110	Amazing Secrets Video & Book	$49.95	_____
_____	1929194129	Amazing Secrets CD Set & Book	$39.95	_____

_____Total # Titles   Total Retail: $_____

Less Discount (See previous page.): $_____

Credit Card Information   Total: $_____
(Visa, MasterCard, or   Shipping charges are added to Total.
American Express only.)   Shipping is UPS Ground FOB Seattle.

Name on Card: _____ .

Card Address:_____

City, State, Zip:_____

Credit Card Number:_____

Expiration Date:_____ Signature:_____

The Warrior Class Training Site
FREE to Clearbridge Book Owners ONLY!
On-line Training in Sun Tzu's Methods

FREE 300-Page E-Book: *The Warrior Class.* In this
e-book, each stanza of *The Art of War* is explained in
detail. Available on-line in Acrobat format.

FREE Slide Shows: Fourteen free slide shows, one
for each chapter of *The Art of War* plus an overview.
Over 300 HTML slides.

FREE Self-scoring Tests: Two tests on each chapter,
one on the text and one on the concepts in *The Warrior
Class* e-book.

PASSWORDS are contained in this book for
accessing The Warrior Class.

Go to www.clearbridge.com/training-area.htm
for the User ID and page number in this book
with the current password.